DIVEЯSION

DIVERSION

GABRIELLE MANDER

First published in Great Britain by Virgin Books Ltd
Thames Wharf Studios
Rainville Road
London W6 9HA

A catalogue record of this book is available from the British Library.

ISBN 978 0 7535 1144 2

The paper used in this book is a natural, recyclable product made from wood grown in
sustainable forests. The manufacturing process conforms to the regulations of the country
of origin.

Designed and typeset by Design 23
Printed and bound in Great Britain by CPD, Wales.

CONTENTS

For
Anthea Campbell who inspired this book

INTRODUCTION

You keep checking in store windows in case your skirt is tucked into your panties or your fly is undone. It wouldn't surprise you to find that your family has moved out and left no forwarding address. You can hardly bring yourself to smile at the attractive guy or girl who picked up your dry cleaning from the oily puddle where you dropped it. Life does not seem to have been going your way lately, and you can't see the wood for the trees. You have lost your sparkle and no amount of light-reflecting make-up can disguise it.

Diversion is a completely original way to beat those common or garden blue days, without the aid of chocolate, hip-hugging ice cream, a hideous haircut, drugs, alcohol, or losing all your friends, by calling them at 3 am after a tequila slammer or two. Blue days can just descend from that silver lining less cloud hanging just above your head, (and yours alone) bringing gloom and doom in their wake.

We all have days like these (no no-one ever told us there would be of course!) or even weeks, when we start racking our brains to recall ladders we might have walked under, or black cats that crossed our paths the wrong way. Some of us even resort to searching our partner's pockets for voodoo dolls.

The unique concept of this book is for all those times when we need to turn a corner, change direction, shake off the glums and get on with our otherwise great lives. 150 21st century plots, ciphers, cryptic puzzles, sudoku, kakuro, hadjie, slitherlink and hitori, games, quests, codes, mysteries and tricks are included, to help you use your brain to divert *yourself* from feeling in a rut, unloved, unappreciated, bored and restless, and put *yourself* in the proper frame of mind to see the opportunities and joys that are just in front of your nose. You will be amazed, it really works and you don't need a lifestyle guru. You don't need to invite a television crew to make over your home badly either. You don't need cosmetic procedures. You just need your own unique talents, native intelligence, common sense and a sense of humour.

The common sense: There is a difference between feeling down and serious depression. If your symptoms are prolonged, and for no discernible reason and are coupled with difficulties in eating or sleeping, and an inability to face everyday life, please consult a doctor.

But for those glass half-empty days, this book echoes with the irritating voice of experience. It will take you through simple visualisation and breathing and positive thinking exercises that won't drive your friends away even faster than the 3 am 'I really love you, you are my best friend' technique. Practical hot tips for every situation are given too, to help you on your way. Then comes the fun part - the diversions. They will help you through the down times or take the edge of the boredom of waiting for something to happen to change your life. They can also give you a bit of breathing space to get your real life problems in perspective. Exercising your brain to solve puzzles and conundrums improves your natural-born ability to solve real dilemmas, like how to improve that dead-end job or fill a holiday weekend when there's no one to share with, or the feeling that life has passed you by now that the kids have left home.

You can use any of the diversions in this book at any time, even though some are especially designed for particular situations. Pretty soon challenges become opportunities and that glass will always be half full. It must be admitted that some of the diversions are very silly. Humour makes almost any situation better, even if you are only laughing on the inside or up your sleeve. Nothing in this book is a test of your intelligence or a competition to see who wins. It's simple, you always win.

Diversion is for everyone who has ever had a bad day, who has kissed a lot of frogs and come up prince-less, who didn't win the lottery (again), whose favourite trousers just shrunk in the closet and whose dog was sick on the papers needed for this morning's vital meeting. But it is also for people who love to use their brain to divert themselves to ascend the downward spiral, by solving mysteries, cracking codes, writing stories, learning new and useless skills or trying any of the other creative diversions contained herein.

Finally, if you get too frustrated, the solutions to the mathematical and wordsearch diversions, and the mystery in the middle are to be found at the back of the book. So as my father used to say 'Let's get cracking.' One word of warning, if your friends start to call you Pollyanna, you've gone too far!

BACK TO BASICS

When you are feeling in the dumps it can be very difficult to see beyond the misery of the moment. However, it is extraordinary how useful mastering a few basic techniques can be in helping you to get out from under. Controlling your breathing can help you to take control of your body, which is especially important when you are feeling helpless. Using your breath to direct your body's energy increases the oxygen in your bloodstream, improves your concentration and helps to calm angst. There are many good books which teach us the value of deep breathing exercises in detoxing the body and controlling both pain and pleasure; breath control is an important part of Tantric sex for example. In everyday life, controlling our breathing can help us to achieve physical and emotional calm and balance. The following exercises are very simple. If you want to learn more complex techniques, you could do worse than enrol in yoga class. The first thing you will be taught is to be aware of your breathing. Yoga can also teach you to bring your physical and emotional aspects into harmony. (No more mind, body and spirit I promise, but, with all the zeal of a recent convert, I can tell you that it works.)

Take a deep breath

1. Stand up straight, or lie on your back, hands held loosely at your sides, palms up and shoulders relaxed with feet slightly apart (about hip-width).

2. Take a deep breath in through your nose, and as you inhale push out your abdomen as your chest rises. Hold it for a count of three.

3. Breathe out really slowly, through your mouth, pulling your abdomen in first.

Repeat five times.

The trick is to do it slowly. If you rush, you will simply hyperventilate and feel dizzy.

While you are thinking about that pressing worry or trying to work out how you feel and what you really want, it can be difficult to unwind and to get into the frame of mind when you can make sensible decisions or face inevitable change. Sleep can prove elusive too, but these simple exercises can help. It is important to be comfortable, dim the lights and make sure you are warm enough and not in a draught. Combining relaxation and breathing exercises will make both all the more effective. You can also relax in a warm bath. If you feel that soothing music helps, play it quietly. One of those CDs of classical music for babies works perfectly well for grown-ups, if whale song, or the turning of the tide is not to your taste. (The sound of the sea or a waterfall can make you feel fidgety!)

Just relax

1. Lie down on your back on a bed, or the floor with your feet slightly raised and about hip-width apart, with a comfortable pillow beneath your head, hands held loosely by your sides, with palms upward. Take five deep breaths, as above.

2. Close your eyes and concentrate your attention on your toes. You are going to tense and relax all the muscles in your body in turn, from the toes upward. Try to think of nothing but your breathing. Inhale as you tense the muscles and exhale as you relax them.

3. Curl your toes as hard as you can, hold for five seconds, and then relax them. In your head say 'relax my toes' in a soothing voice, as they

relax. Then, tighten the muscles in your feet and ankles, then relax them saying 'relax my feet and ankles', then your calves, thighs, tummy, buttocks (this will also aid firm buttocks, but that is another story), fingers, wrists and arms, diaphragm, shoulders neck and face. Every part of you is tensed and relaxed in turn, until even your hair feels relaxed. Breathe out slowly through your mouth as you do so. Lie still and calm and relaxed for five minutes. Do not leap up immediately.

Relaxation-lite

If you are in a public place, and you don't want to blow your cool or burst into tears, you might feel a little silly doing a full relaxation exercise. Although if done discreetly, you need not sacrifice the clenching and relaxing of the buttocks part, so the firming bonus can still be yours. However, most of the physical tension of emotional angst is seated further up, in your face, neck and shoulders. The quickest way to release it is as follows.

1. Take a deep breath, and drop your shoulders whilst breathing out. Continue to breath out through your nose, shallow breaths, not deep ones.

2. Turn your palms upward and open them out, resting them lightly on your thighs (if seated). Resist clenching your hands or wringing them, or gripping the arms of a chair. Keep breathing gently.

3. If seated, keep your feet flat on the floor, don't cross your knees or ankles.

4. Raise your eyebrows (not like Groucho Marx, just lift them gently, those who have received botox can imagine their eyebrows lifted) and most importantly, smile. I know you don't feel like it, but just give it a try; this need not be a toothpaste grin, more the secret smile of the Mona Lisa. Don't worry, strangers will go away muttering, 'There is a woman or man of mystery'. If the situation is appropriate, laughing is even more effective, but self-tickling doesn't work and asking a stranger to tickle you may result in unforeseen consequences, but it's your choice.

5. If you feel yourself beginning to tense up, take a deep breath and start again.

Seeing is believing

This is not a book about meditation, but it is true that anticipating a positive outcome can contribute to its success. Accentuate the positive, eliminate the negative and don't mess with Mr In-Between, as the old song would have it. It is all to easy to believe that nothing can ever change, that you don't deserve to be happier or more fulfilled. Don't even think it.

Instead, when you need to make a change in your life, prepare by doing any research you may need into the alternatives to your current situation. Then when you are calm and relaxed, perhaps after completing the exercises above, look around you and choose an object on which to concentrate, a flower, or a picture perhaps. In a minute, you are going to close your eyes and see that object in your mind's eye. Anything will do, but it needs to be a strong enough image for you to retain it. You know that if you look at a light, the sun perhaps, or a bedside lamp just before you turn it out, and then close your eyes, the image is retained for a few moments, well that is what we are looking for, so if you have a candle handy, light it and just look at it for a few moments.

Concentrate on the light, the way it flickers, and then close your eyes. Hold the image of the light, or the object you have chosen, in your mind's eye. If you lose concentration, just open your eyes and start again. Now look into the heart of the light or the object, breathing gently and as the image fades, picture a happier you who gets a little less of the low-fat spread and a little more of the full-fat cream in life.

Let's take tackling your boss about that promotion as an example. See yourself, relaxed and confident talking to your line manager, you are smiling; he or she is smiling. She is pleased to see you and open to your suggestions. You stand and shake hands and thank her for her time. She tells you how delighted the company is with your progress and that she will consider your proposal very seriously. You smile and say that you are open to any other suggestions that she may have. You leave, knowing that you have conducted yourself well and are in the frame of mind that will allow you to consider your position very carefully when all consultations are concluded. Now open your eyes. Keep thinking positively.

Like most skills, successful visualisation takes practice. You probably have a lifetime of negative thinking to overcome. You may need to do the exercise a couple of times to maintain concentration. Do not let negative thoughts and nasty, nagging doubts creep in. There is absolutely no reason why this should not be the outcome. This technique does work, but it isn't magic. Nothing will help if you have shown no interest in your job, take too many duvet days, and allow disappointment to persuade you to give less than one-hundred percent. But provided, too that you have done your preparation thoroughly, only your own negativity stands in the way of success. It is about control, not spell-casting. If you are relaxed and positive it will communicate itself to others. A friend once told me you get what you expect, not what you deserve. To a degree that's probably true, but I prefer to think that you can get what you expect and deserve.

If you say negative things to yourself, you reinforce low expectations, and that also communicates itself to others. You do deserve to be happier and more fulfilled. You are clever, capable and loveable. If you have spent a lifetime telling yourself or being told otherwise, you may need to work a little harder on your self-esteem. Try simple affirmations, telling yourself that you can, rather than can't. Remember the little engine that could? If you repeat encouraging positive phrases to yourself before you go to sleep, you will wake up feeling empowered. A friend of mine writes affirming statements on sticky notes and puts them all over her house. It works for her.

You now have new skills to help boost your self-esteem and promote positive thinking, but there may still be those hours to fill. Don't panic, they will fly by and you will beat the blues with the diversions in the following pages.

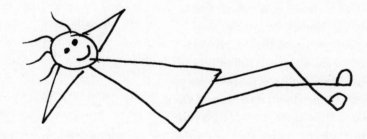

DEAD-END JOB

Have you been passed over for promotion once too often? Do you feel unappreciated, while your friends seem to be flying high in their great, executive jobs? Perhaps you only took this job as a short-term measure and you are still there three years later? Maybe it is not a job that allows the real you to develop your full potential and your boss can't see that? Or are you just feeling bored and restless and want to make a change in your life? Do you

think that changing your job will solve all your money, relationship or social life problems at a stroke? Does any of this sound familiar? You are not alone, and you may well be right that a career change is what you need, but what if this is just one of those days when you and your boss are out of sync? You might feel completely differently about it all tomorrow? Before you text your resignation to HR, or suggest politely where your manager might like to stick this job, take a little time to think about what you really want and feel. There probably do need to be some changes made, but they may not be as drastic as you imagine. If you still feel the same in 24 hours time, go for it, but make sure that the move you make is in the right direction. If your boss is a bully or doesn't respond to your sensible, positive efforts, it is time for a change anyway. Here are some ideas while you are thinking, which might help you to make a constructive move this time.

HOT TIPS

Before...

Never burn your bridges! The short-term satisfaction of telling people what you think of them is outweighed by the possible need for references later.

Write a letter or email to your boss, venting all your emotions about your current situation, but DON'T send it. This is like shouting down a well, it clears your head without harming your prospects.

Take a large piece of paper and make a list of where you are in your present job; salary, prospects, job satisfaction, colleagues, ease of travel, perks, potential for promotion, and or change etc. Include all the pros and cons. Try to be fair, even if you are seriously fed-up. Now make a second list alongside the first, of where you had hoped to be by now, including your dreams and fantasies. Don't leave anything out because you feel that those early ambitions were unattainable. So what if you are at the check-out and you wanted to be a sky-diving nun! Now make a third list, of where you would like to be in three years time. These lists are just for you, so be honest! Now go away and leave the lists for a while and try a diversion. When you come back, review the lists and make any changes or additions. How far away are you from your dreams? Now you need to be straightforward about your future hopes. Is there a possibility that with training you can achieve some of them in your current job? Is it a stepping-stone in the right direction?

If so, make an appointment with your line manager to discuss your prospects in detail. Now make a new list of where you want to go in your career. Be brave and positive. Prepare a list of questions for your existing or any new employer about any vacancies on offer. Make sure that any step you take will bring you closer to your dreams.

Make a list of your assets. Think about what you have to offer to your employer, as well as want you want from your job. Ask really close, trusted friends what they think of as your special qualities and talents.

Scan on-line job vacancies and wanted ads in the newspaper to see if there are jobs out there which match your criteria. Research any companies, which seem to operate in the areas in which you are interested.

Research any training courses available within your chosen area, which could give you extra qualifications to help your prospects for promotion.

Write your own perfect job description.

Take an on-line or night school course in preparing a CV or resumé. Review all your interests and achievements and create a new document to show your existing or prospective employer.

Take a look at yourself. Could your image or attitude do with a little updating too?

Think positive. You deserve to spend your time doing something which satisfies the whole you, if at all possible. If this seems unlikely, for financial reasons, take a look at the rest of your life. Are there areas where you fulfil some of the needs you have identified, outside working hours?

Take control and take your time. Create a timetable for change that suits you and move towards it with confidence. You have done a considerable amount of research, about how you could make a difference to your company and improve your life.
Remember make your own positive suggestions, don't just say, 'Bored now, make it better.' Show how well you know the company you work for. Is there a job swap you could do within the organisation? Would you accept a pay cut for a more challenging role? Is there training available to improve the job you have? Make sure you really know what you want, and that it is to the benefit of both the company and you, then ask for it, confidently and charmingly.

Remember you deserve a happier and more fulfilling role at work. Before any interview or conversation with your boss, do the visualisation exercises on page 16, or use the following scenario: Close your eyes and imagine that you have opened the door, gone inside and sat down, you are smiling, (naturally, not inanely), Your boss is smiling, you are both receptive to a positive outcome. Your boss is impressed by the work and preparation you have done, even if you can't get what you want immediately, this meeting will help you on your way. You are shaking hands and things are on the up. If you start to lose confidence, try those positive affirmations before you go to sleep.

Never photocopy any part of your anatomy!

Never burn bridges. Yes, I know that was number one, but it bears repeating. While you consider all your options try some or all of the diversions that follow.

DIVEЯSION

Write an acrostic poem

Use your current job title as a basis. You will be amazed at what it could reveal about your real dreams. Try to think of words that actually apply to you. If this doesn't work for you with a job title, use your name instead. Examples:

RECEPTIONIST
Really Exciting Career?
Excellent Pleaser,
Too Intelligent? Over-Nice?
I Should Triumph

MECHANIC
Maybe Everyone Can Have A Night In Cuba

MARIE
Marvellous Asset Rarely Inspires Envy

SUDOKU

Place the numbers 1 to 9 into the grid so that each row, column and marked 3x3 box contains each number once and once only.

Hint: Start by looking for numbers that can fit in only one place in a row, column or 3x3 box.

DIVE**Я**SION

Write a short story

(2000 words) The story must begin ...

EITHER ...

She sat at the table, scanning the wanted ads in the newspaper; 'Relief milker wanted, no previous experience needed'; 'Kind compassionate carer to house sit, must love crocodiles'; 'Chief Executive, Pharmaceutical Company', 'Chorus girl,' 'Night watchman', 'Dog walker,' 'Sausage-maker'. Who, she wondered woke up one morning and thought to themselves, 'There must be a job for my special skills, where I can really use my love of crocodiles?' This was hopeless; she really didn't know what she wanted to do, only that she hated what she was doing now. Emma had drifted into this job as a government clerk, because that was what was expected of her. It was safe and secure with good, if slow prospects for promotion, a solid pension, assisted mortgage etc etc. – perfect – perfectly dull. So far, Mr Right had not bumped into her one morning, spilling her coffee and then as he tried in vain to brush away the spill from her blouse, meeting her eyes, and realising that she was not just another girl in the office. Some chance in pod world!

As a child she craved excitement and adventure, she was known as the brave and fearless one. How had she ended up chained to a pc all day long and for the foreseeable future? Her eyes roamed the columns idly and there it was: Do you crave excitement and adventure? Are you known as the brave and fearless one? Box no 30782...

OR...

Okay, so he had not told her the whole truth, he was not actually head of an award-winning advertising agency, but he could just tell, as he bought this creamy-skinned, tawny beauty a drink at the bar, that 'dentist' wasn't going to cut it. She had crossed her apparently endless legs and flashed him a smile that he would have been proud to have helped create. She ran a red-tipped finger up the frosted glass of her indescribable drink and leaned a little towards him. 'That's fantastic', she said, 'I'm a model, and I am so looking for a mentor to help me break into the big time.' She could, he thought, be the new face of

Calvin Klein or Estee Lauder, or anyone, she was so incredibly beautiful. She wriggled a little with delight. 'Can you really make that happen?' she cooed. My God, had he said that out loud? Did he even know anyone in advertising? Jake searched his mental Rolodex, imagining it sitting neatly next to the sterilizer back at the office. Desperately, he wondered if he could yet win her with a ride in his state of the art dentist's chair and a swill of mouthwash? Suddenly, he saw it, neatly typed on the card, Jake Monroe, Hanover, Ingoldby, Frantz, Advertising Executive. His patient even had the same first name. This was only semi-identity theft. 'I'll see what I can do' he said, as she wrote her number on the matchbook...

WORDSEARCH: Dream jobs

DIVE⅁SION

```
B L I V R Y D N G D M O N J L
R N A O J E C A R I R U Z R E
X A T W N U T I R E R N E J D
R C T T Y I V C T S H K G U O
A E I S Z E C I E D A C L D M
Y S M C R Y R T X M A D A G X
T O Y A I W O I M D S F E E M
K C O R T P I L O T T R D D T
T A W J G N I O H W R E O J R
R E C I F F O P V F O C C W W
O E X E C U T I V E N N T H V
A R T I S T Q R L Q A A O E D
B E C I L O P L A Y U D R N X
C N L N G H P T X I T O I F S
R Q W L T B T M R F N Y E A E
```

ACTOR
ARTIST
ASTRONAUT
DANCER
DENTIST
DOCTOR
EXECUTIVE
FILMMAKER
JUDGE
LAWYER
LION-TAMER
MODEL
NURSE
PILOT
POLICE/OFFICER
POLITICIAN
ROCK/STAR
TEACHER
TRAIN/DRIVER
WRITER

ACRONYMS

The following acronyms all relate to the world of work. Can you guess what they mean, or create new meanings for them?

AAPNAC
AONAO
CRAFT
DIN
DRIB
EBOM
GROW
KASH
MBWA
NAP
SEP
SUMO
SWOT
USP
WYGIWYE

DIVERSION

Imagine what the man in the picture is saying or thinking
and fill in the speech bubbles.

DIVEЯSION

HANJIE

Shade in squares to reveal a hidden picture. The clue numbers to the top and left reveal how many adjacent shaded squares there are in each column and row respectively. If there are multiple numbers for a row or column then there are multiple sequences of adjacent shaded squares with at least one empty square between them, in the order given. For example, "2, 3" would mean that somewhere in that row or column there are 2 adjacent shaded squares, followed by a gap of one or more squares, followed by 3 adjacent shaded squares.

Hint: It's essential to mark in squares you know to be empty with a dot or cross, otherwise you will find it very hard to solve this puzzle! A good tactic is to start by considering the rows and columns with the most shaded squares.

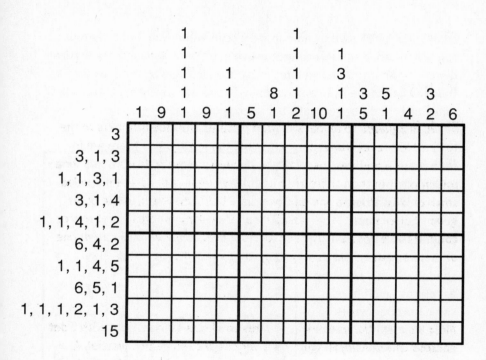

HITORI

Shade in squares so that no number occurs more than once per row or column. Shaded squares cannot touch in either a horizontal or vertical direction. All unshaded squares must form a single continuous area so that you can move from any unshaded square to any other by travelling only horizontally or vertically between them.

Hint: Circle numbers which must be unshaded in order to keep track of your progress and help see which numbers must be shaded. Start by looking for places where the same number occurs close to itself in a row or column, and considering if anything can be deduced from this.

8	8	4	6	6	3	5	1
1	2	7	5	7	4	7	6
7	8	6	1	4	2	8	1
5	6	3	2	4	8	3	7
4	1	2	7	8	6	7	3
5	7	5	3	5	1	6	4
6	5	8	7	1	6	2	3
3	4	3	1	3	2	3	5

CANCELLED FLIGHT

We have all experienced it. The holiday plans ruined because of airline difficulties, security alerts or industrial action. Somehow, a cancelled flight seems more disastrous and significant than a delayed train or a car breakdown. Perhaps it is because the anticipation is so much greater. Planes promise to take us out of ourselves, as well as away from our humdrum lives.

The planning and packing and arriving hours before take-off, at locations that are frequently inconvenient to us loom large. The bustle and officialdom and nowadays the fear of security problems ratchet up our anxiety levels, so that the natural adrenalin surge at the excitement of getting away from it all for a fortnight in the sun, or a business meeting in a sophisticated city far away, morphs into grumpiness and nervous anticipation.

Almost all of us over the age of ten arrive at the airport with full suitcases and a glass half-empty attitude. If customs unpack your suitcase will you ever get everything back in? Did you pack the vital papers for the meeting and horror of horrors will your flight be delayed or even cancelled so that your world will collapse? Somehow we find ourselves taking personal responsibility for ill fortune. If my flight is cancelled and I don't make the meeting in New York, I will be fired. (Of course you won't, you can't control international airline schedules.) Will they put me on another flight, which will stop over in some foreign airport for which I have not prepared myself with a list of unnecessary worries? Will I lose my hotel reservation and have to sleep in a box under the railway arches? Will my luggage go to Timbuktu whilst I arrive in Glasgow? I hope your luggage labels read Ms or Mr Pessimist, No Hope Hotel.

Yes cancelled flights are a drag, but it is not the end of the world. A few precautions taken in advance can ease the anxiety and lift the gloom if you have a long wait at the airport. When that annoying PA system announces your flight is cancelled, take a more pragmatic view.

HOT TIPS

Take a list in your hand luggage with all-important contact numbers in red ink or arrange a list on your mobile phone. Contact anyone who is expecting your arrival, business colleagues, hotel reservations, chauffeur services etc, immediately to let them know of the delay. Keep them updated on your progress. Many airports have Internet and email facilities if you don't have a mobile phone to text your hosts. If there is a time difference at your destination, which makes it difficult to make contact, phone someone at your place of departure and ask him or her to contact those expecting you at a more convenient time. Let your family or friends know of your delay or they will worry.

If there is a long line at the information desk, telephone or email the main switchboard of your carrier for updated information.

Make sure you have plenty of bottled water, and slow release carbohydrate snacks like cereal bars with you. These are better for you and the kids if you are travelling as family. Avoid too much coffee, all alcohol and sugary snacks. That being said, travel as light as possible.

Wear loose comfortable clothes to travel in, you can always change when you get there.

If feasible, take a lightweight blanket or pashmina to combat airport air conditioning and an inflatable pillow.

Find the biggest, fattest, most escapist novel you can in the airport bookstore. If at all possible find somewhere to sit. Now you can enjoy your wait.

If you are travelling with children, pack some coloured crayons and drawing paper and reading materials for them.

If it is a business trip, pack any work documents as easily accessible hand luggage. Catch up on the paperwork you had planned to do on the flight. Now you will be able to relax and enjoy the movie.

It is the airline's job to sort this problem. Once you have the information you need, do the relaxation-lite exercises on page 14 and await developments patiently. Try to make the best of the situation. Can you help anyone more anxious than you, perhaps someone travelling alone with children or who is less well prepared? It will make you feel better.

If your new flight is to be diverted via another country and your stopover will allow you to get off the plane, buy a guidebook to that country and plan a small excursion.

Think positive, you have contacted those expecting you, so use your time to relax and reflect, or perhaps make new friends or business contacts.

Try some of the following diversions to pass the time.

DIVE**Я**SION

Write a short story

(2000 words) The story must begin...

EITHER . . .

Karolyn awoke gasping for breath in the silence of the night. The room seemed oppressively close after the gentle night breeze coming off the grey-green sea of her dream. Her skin felt clammy with sweat, where moments before it had been bathed in the light sea-spray carried on the wind. The greenish illumination of the figures on her alarm clock blinked the hour, 2.31. It had seemed to her, as she had stood at the water's edge, that time was irrelevant in the gentle, grey moonlight. She had felt such a sense of complete peace and harmony. Now the anxiety of the inevitable insomnia that would follow her abrupt awakening began to tease her. What had pulled her from her deep sleep? She lay listening in the darkness for any sound that could have penetrated her sub-conscious. Her heart began to beat a little faster, but she could hear nothing but the pulse thrumming gently in her ears. Perhaps, in this remote country place, the cry of a night animal long since gone on its way had disturbed her. Perhaps someone had tried to break in. Her heart began to race as she reached for the light switch and swung her legs out of bed. Was that a creak on the stair? As her bare feet reached the soft carpet and searched automatically for her slippers, she glanced downward and her frantic heart missed a beat. It couldn't be, there on the carpet, a damp footprint and soft sand between her toes...

OR . . .

Thomas did not perspire; His face was never suffused with a blush of exertion or embarrassment. His pulse was barely discernible at the monthly check-up required by his 'employers'. Nothing ruffled his pale corn-coloured hair, greying now at the temples. No expression on his clean-cut, handsome face revealed his thoughts or feelings. Nothing marred the perfect line of his Armani suit. No scuff or speck of dust touched his highly polished Italian shoes. His perfectly knotted burgundy tie met the sharp points of his spotless white shirt collar at a precise angle. The smile he now directed at the clerk behind the airline desk didn't disturb the steeliness of his grey eyes with any touch of warmth or humour. The man shifted uncomfortably in his swivel chair and adjusted his own professional manner. Thomas inclined his six - foot frame imperceptibly towards the clerk. He did not bother to voice the question, but slightly raised a quizzical eyebrow as he presented his documents. The clerk began to punch information into his computer, feeling unaccountably intimidated by the quiet assurance of the man that seemed to say. 'Just give me the solution to this problem; no excuses, no explanations; just the new flight details and the upgrade to first class that is my due.' And all without uttering a word. The clerk began to sweat, as the screen failed to provide the instant response this man would undoubtedly require. The noisy, anxious family behind Thomas in the line disturbed the clerk's concentration. Thomas stood perfectly still and looked into his eyes. The sweat began to cool on the clerk's upper lip and the hairs on the back of his neck began to rise...

WORDSEARCH: Cancelled Flight   DIVE**Я**SION

```
L  E  P  L  U  B  N  A  T  S  I  D  S  E  R
F  A  U  A  X  A  O  R  G  Y  W  A  P  R  O
S  D  E  G  R  G  A  I  C  U  L  D  U  A  T
U  T  L  R  A  I  W  P  E  L  C  I  L  E  C
T  L  M  C  T  R  S  B  A  M  O  N  S  J  Y
F  Q  I  L  N  N  P  D  A  K  O  I  B  A  S
S  H  Z  O  Q  B  O  D  A  N  L  R  U  M  N
C  T  R  N  R  D  R  M  R  A  G  T  A  G  I
K  O  Z  D  V  I  S  Q  B  C  H  K  I  D  A
R  K  V  O  D  T  S  Y  D  N  E  Y  O  P  B
O  Y  J  N  E  T  O  R  O  N  T  O  C  K  M
Y  O  K  R  N  O  B  S  I  L  D  A  P  Q  U
Y  U  D  N  E  W  H  A  R  F  I  G  P  X  M
X  A  F  X  N  P  Y  P  I  R  B  G  X  X  W
M  J  A  M  S  N  B  E  O  N  S  T  J  J  Y
```

AMSTERDAM
BALI
BANGKOK
CAIRO
CHICAGO
DALLAS
ISTANBUL
LISBON
LONDON
MADRID
MONTREAL
MUMBAI
NEW/YORK
PARIS
PRAGUE
ROME
SYDNEY
TOKYO
TORONTO
TRINIDAD

HITORI

Shade in squares so that no number occurs more than once per row or column. Shaded squares cannot touch in either a horizontal or vertical direction. All unshaded squares must form a single continuous area so that you can move from any unshaded square to any other by travelling only horizontally or vertically between them.

Hint: Circle numbers which must be unshaded in order to keep track of your progress and help see which numbers must be shaded. Start by looking for places where the same number occurs close to itself in a row or column, and considering if anything can be deduced from this.

6	8	6	2	4	5	7	7
7	7	6	7	2	8	3	1
3	4	4	8	5	4	2	7
4	5	3	6	1	1	3	4
1	8	5	4	6	4	8	3
7	2	4	1	1	3	1	6
2	2	7	5	8	5	4	5
7	6	8	3	1	5	1	2

45

IRREGULAR SUDOKU

Place the numbers 1 to 9 into the grid so that each row, column and bold shape contains each number once and once only.

Hint: You can sometimes use the widest part of each shape, and the way in which it overlaps with a row or column, to help eliminate possibilities.

		9		8		7		
		2	6		5	1		
6		5				2		1
4		7				5		9
		1	2		3	8		
		4		9		3		

46

KAKURO

Place only the numbers 1 to 9 into the empty white squares so that each across or down run of white squares adds up to the total above or to the left of it. No number can be used more than once in any run, so you cannot use 2 and 2 to add up to '4'. Numbers to the right of the diagonal line give the sum of squares to the right; numbers below the diagonal line give the sum of squares below.

Hint: Start by looking for runs of white squares where only one set of digits will fit, such as 16 (7 and 9) or 17 (8 and 9).

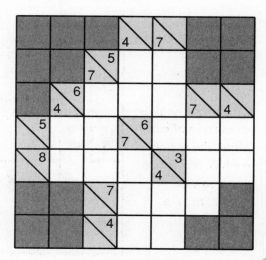

REBUS PUZZLES

The design of the type and its position in the box gives a clue to its meaning which will be a well-known phrase or saying.

RI   BS

WON

    ONE

WON

E		E
	Y	
E		E

RA
AM
CP
EM

FLYER

LIFE11TIME

MOVING ON

Your landlord is selling your perfect rent-controlled apartment. You are leaving home for the first time to set up home alone. The breakdown of a relationship means that you have to move out and move on. On the positive side perhaps you are getting married, or moving in with the love of your life, or a fabulous new job involves relocation. Maybe your family is growing and you need more space. Even in these happy circumstances, insurance statistics tell us that moving house is second only to bereavement as a major cause of stress and unhappiness. The more baggage you are carrying, literally and metaphorically, the more stressful the experience. How can you maximise the pleasure in such a traumatic change and minimise the pain?

It is really important that you feel that your destination has more to offer than your current home. That doesn't mean that it needs to be bigger, more expensive and have a more exclusive address. But it probably means that you should be very sure that this move is what you want, or a real step on the way to it. You may have to be dragged, kicking and screaming from the building, after the bolt cutters have been used to sever the chains attached at one end to your wrist, and at the other, to the lavatory. But whilst you may have no choice but to move out, you have limitless choices about how you move on. That's all very fine and dandy, but what about my limited budget? I hear you mutter darkly. The important thing is to expand your choices within the inevitable constraints of cash and location and to make sure that your next home is going to be the place in which you have the best chance of happiness. Also try to squeeze the most pleasure from the process.

HOT TIPS

Keep an open mind! That houseboat or lighthouse may not be out of the question.

Before you lift the phone to the agents or scan the rental and for sale ads, take a large piece of paper and draw up a list of your ideal requirements for your dream home. Use your imagination and don't hold back. Don't persuade yourself that there is no hope of you getting it so there is no point in dreaming. Start with what is most important to you. Do you crave a lively, transient neighbourhood with restaurants, bars, clubs and cinemas, or a quiet one with an established community? Do you hope to make new friends or be closer to existing ones? Do you need green spaces to refresh your spirits or are you happy in an urban landscape? Think about who you would like to be and how you would like to live, rather than how you live now. Are you prepared to decorate or renovate? This is a wish list and it helps to clear your head and start to focus on the positive aspects of moving on.

Now write another list, with the things that are absolutely fixed. Ease of travel to work, or proximity to schools might feature. So might the possibility of keeping a pet, a little bit of garden or ease of access, security, or financial constraints. Once again be honest and free. Look at the lists side-by-side and cross out anything on the second list which is not absolutely essential. Highlight everything on the first list that gives you a little tingle of excitement when you imagine it.

Compose the imaginary estate agents details for this dream home, including all the absolute requirements and the essential assets. Keep this by you at all times in the search for the perfect home.

Don't settle for a dark cupboard in a desirable neighbourhood, when you could have a light and airy space in a less sought-after one.

If funds are limited, consider sharing space or letting a room. It can be a way to make new friends as well as cover the rent or mortgage. Watch out for single, white, female syndrome and always take up references.

Draw up a timetable for finding a new place, signing up or exchanging contracts and moving in, while you are still in control of the operation. Be realistic but positive.

Prepare a budget to cover all the expenses involved in moving. Include insurance, possible temporary accommodation, removal costs, professional fees etc.

Make a list of the things that need to be done like closing utility accounts and opening new ones, forwarding mail, notifying friends and relations of your new address etc.

Research areas in which you think you would like to live. There are often neighbourhood websites, which tell you about facilities in the immediate vicinity, but if at all possible, go and look around yourself.

Have a few meals in local restaurants, browse the local stores, travel by public transport and keep an open mind. If you can, take a friend along.

This is part of the adventure, not a military exercise.

Never take agent's details at face value, always check for yourself and learn to translate agent-speak. This can be fun. 'Development potential', for example, means major building work. 'Close to organic food sources' could mean next door to a pig farm.

If you are buying, make sure all local searches are done, Check local planning applications including those for road re-routing or major utility works.

When you have found your new home, get estimates for removals including packing. There is nothing more depressing than a dozen exhausting car trips with wobbly boxes because you thought you could do this yourself.

Clear out unwanted items ruthlessly. This is a chance to detox your life, do not pack five box loads of old letters, records, clothes or knick-knacks that bind you to your previous life.

Don't just recreate your old home in your new space. Look at loads of magazines and brochures before you decide on your décor. Everything does not have to be done at once. Sometimes it is a good idea to live in a space for a month before you remodel or redecorate.

Remember this is somewhere you will want to invite your new and old friends to visit; it is your chance to express your personality.

If you have to decorate your new place, consider a painting party. Invite your most competent friends to wield a paintbrush accompanied by music, drinks and a take-away. Again it can be fun and helps invest your new home with the most positive aspects of your life.

Try to stay with friends or splash out on a luxury night in a hotel on the last night before your move. There is nothing more gloomy than sleeping in an empty house with all your possessions tied in a spotted handkerchief.

On moving day, make sure you keep one box aside with a kettle, mugs, coffee, tea, milk, sugar, spoon, a bottle of wine, glasses, a corkscrew and luxury chocolate cookies, nuts and olives packed inside. Also keep the bed linen you are going to need out of the main packing. When you reach your new home you will at least be able to have a drink and make up a bed before you attack the unpacking. If you arrive late in the afternoon or evening, don't even think about unpacking. Go out and have a meal, and then have a long hot bath before you go to bed. Start fresh in the morning.

Buy yourself flowers and put them in a vase or jar at your new home as soon as you arrive.

Introduce yourself to your new neighbours; invite them in for coffee or a drink. Smile be friendly and confident, but don't tell them your life story or all your woes at first meeting.

Walk about your new neighbourhood and try to experience one new thing every week.

Don't look back. This is your present and your future and it can be great if you want it to be.

If you make a mistake, swallow your pride and move again! While you wait for the removal men, electrician, agent, or locksmith divert yourself!

WORDSEARCH: Moving on

DIVER**SION**

```
G G Y R I S N D E L R L F O Z
N P U D O E U L E O D E R P X
I L A W E N E R M C J V I P J
S F A M I L Y A P E O A E O A
N J Z R H X N W X R N R N R D
A Q G O E C H C E Y I T D T W
E N M M E G I F R N J S S U M
L E E R U T N E V D A R E N L
C E K C E A V E W K E U B I O
O E G M I O I R L E O D D T V
Q T E N C U U E R L R Q Y Y E
B N M S A A H A N S A Q U K G
T X I T G H C L A U G H T E R
Q D B M V Z C B X V O W C S R
F H O A O M R X N U F Q G K Q
```

ADVENTURE
CAREER
CHALLENGE
CHANGE
CLEANSING
DECOR
DISCOVERY
EXCITEMENT
FAMILY
FRIENDS
FUN
HOME
LAUGHTER
LOVE
NEW
OPPORTUNITY
RENEWAL
ROMANCE
SURPRISE
TRAVEL

SLITHERLINK

Draw a single loop by joining the dots with straight horizontal or vertical lines. Each number specifies how many adjacent dots must be joined in the 'square' around that number. Areas without numbers can have any number of dots joined. The loop cannot touch or cross over itself.

Hint: Start by considering the corners and the o and 3 'squares'. Mark the areas between dots that you deduce must not be joined with a small 'x'.

```
.   .   2   .   2   .   1   .   2   .   3   .

.   .   2   .   3   .   1   .   3   .   2   .

.   2   2   2   1   2   .   1   .   .   1   2

.   3   2   2   2   1   .   2   .   .   1   2

.   1   2   .   3   .   2   1   2   2   3   .

.   2   3   .   2   .   2   1   3   1   2   .

.   2   .   1   .   0   .   1   .   3   .   .

.   2   .   1   .   2   .   1   .   2   .   .
```

58

HITORI

Shade in squares so that no number occurs more than once per row or column. Shaded squares cannot touch in either a horizontal or vertical direction. All unshaded squares must form a single continuous area so that you can move from any unshaded square to any other by travelling only horizontally or vertically between them.

Hint: Circle numbers which must be unshaded in order to keep track of your progress and help see which numbers must be shaded. Start by looking for places where the same number occurs close to itself in a row or column, and considering if anything can be deduced from this.

8	3	5	3	6	7	2	2
8	8	7	1	3	1	5	2
4	7	2	5	4	6	3	8
2	5	8	5	1	5	7	3
3	1	2	6	4	5	2	8
1	5	6	3	7	4	8	3
3	4	6	8	6	2	6	5
7	2	1	3	8	4	4	3

SUDOKU

Place the numbers 1 to 9 into the grid so that each row, column and marked 3x3 box contains each number once and once only.

Hint: Start by looking for numbers that can fit in only one place in a row, column or 3x3 box.

				5				
3								9
7	2		9	6	4		3	1
	1						9	
4		7	1		6	8		2
	8						4	
1	9		4	2	3		6	8
8								3
				1				

60

KAKURO

Place only the numbers 1 to 9 into the empty white squares so that each across or down run of white squares adds up to the total above or to the left of it. No number can be used more than once in any run, so you cannot use 2 and 2 to add up to '4'. Numbers to the right of the diagonal line give the sum of squares to the right; numbers below the diagonal line give the sum of squares below.

Hint: Start by looking for runs of white squares where only one set of digits will fit, such as 16 (7 and 9) or 17 (8 and 9).

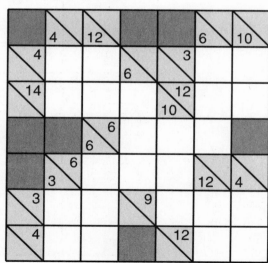

61

AGENT-SPEAK CRYPTOGRAMS

The following words have been coded. The alphabet has been manipulated in each case. Each word features in agent's details for properties and means less than it suggests. Two letters are given to help you crack the code and a single word clue is given for each.

A	B	C	D	E	F	G	H	I	J	K	L	M	N	O	P	Q	R	S	T	U	V	W	X	Y	Z
													B								I				

Clue: Small?   O V W B H K

        - I - 0 - -

A	B	C	D	E	F	G	H	I	J	K	L	M	N	O	P	Q	R	S	T	U	V	W	X	Y	Z
	Q																F								

Clue: Unmodernised?   I B F B E A X U Q

        - - S - - - - - D

A	B	C	D	E	F	G	H	I	J	K	L	M	N	O	P	Q	R	S	T	U	V	W	X	Y	Z
			D							T															

Clue: Strange?   O D N I T R G Q

        - H - - M - - -

A B C D E F G H I J K L M N O P Q R S T U V W X Y Z

      Z   P

Clue: Really tiny?   Z N P M B Z I
                          C — M — — C —

A B C D E F G H I J K L M N O P Q R S T U V W X Y Z

    X   I

Clue: Fussy   O D L A I J I H O
                          — X — — I — I — —

A B C D E F G H I J K L M N O P Q R S T U V W X Y Z

            R   T

Clue: Empty   T R G R T N F R W J
                          M I — I M — — I — —

HOME ALONE

It's Friday night and you have no plans for the weekend. This is not because you are Johnny or Jenny No-mates, but because you were too busy to arrange your social life and now it is too late. All your friends are otherwise engaged and you can't admit that you are not, and ask to join in. (Why not?) You suppose that your family has embarked on a long cruise and that even the cat has checked into someone else's hotel for the duration. Now is not the time to reach for the vodka bottle, make a Scooby snack, hit the chocs and count the inevitable pounds and pimples that will follow. Now is the time to rediscover those dreaded inner resources; to recharge your batteries and do all those things that you can never find the time for. No, I don't mean ironing your pants, unless that would make you happy. What about that foreign film season you wanted to see? (Or even 'Lethal Weapons' 1 to infinity?) How about that luxury home-spa you were going to try, or that new exercise DVD that has been sitting in its case since Christmas because you can't get the plastic wrapper off? Now is the time to try again – getting the outer wrapper off that is. Embark on the programme only if you are sure you will continue. Starting such an enterprise and then giving up on Monday will only depress you. These examples may not have sparked your interest but read on, there could be something here you like. Being by yourself once in a while is not the same as being alone. Do not get down about it please; think positive. At the very least you will be relaxed and smugly together on Monday morning and you could be fitter, better informed, calmer and more confident too. When all else fails try some of the diversions in this chapter or anywhere else in the book. You can exercise your brain whilst eating French fancies and painting your toenails blue or buffing your tattoo.

HOT TIPS

Do not imagine that because you have made no plans, no one loves you anymore. Remember someone you know may be facing the weekend home alone too. You didn't call anyone up either. Pick up the phone and call someone for a chat. Ask about their week.

Alternate 'good' activities like exercise and household chores with indulgences if you feel like it.

Go for a walk in the fresh air, even if you don't have immediate access to glorious countryside or the seashore. Walk in the park, or just around your neighbourhood. You are always rushing about and often don't have time to enjoy your own locale. Look up at the buildings. Interesting architecture is often above first floor level. Explore the byways that are off your normal routes. Go and look up the local records.

Check local papers or the Internet for farmers' or flea markets, you don't have to buy, if funds are short, just looking can be fun. But you could find some delicious organic produce.

Shop carefully in your local market or supermarket for the very best ingredients and cook yourself a truly gourmet meal.

Book a bus trip or train ride to the seaside for the day. Even in winter, sea air is good for you.

Be a tourist in your own town. Visit all the local attractions.

Buy an inflatable punch bag and take out your week's worth of frustration on it.

Look through your address book and write (yes, real letters) to those friends and family that you haven't seen for ages and who aren't in your text and email orbit, or call them up.

Book yourself in for a massage, manicure and pedicure.

Buy yourself a bunch of your favourite flowers.

Have a luxurious, candlelit bath with scented oils.

Bake some bread. Kneading the dough is wonderfully therapeutic and you have something delicious and nutritious to show for it at the end of the weekend. If that sounds too fattening, buy some bake-in-the-oven modelling clay and make a work of art.

Cruise the travel agent or go online and plan a fantastic holiday for yourself.

Volunteer to do something useful for your community. Man a phone line or visit someone who is also by themselves, but maybe can't get around like you can.

Learn a new language on line, or investigate a class that you can take.

Join a dance class; it doesn't matter whether it is rock and roll or tango, tap or salsa. Just do it. Or if that is too advanced, put on your favourite tracks at home and dance around and sing along.

Laugh! If you can't just do it, rent a funny video or read an amusing book or invite a friend to tickle you at the earliest opportunity.

Reorganise your wardrobe or declutter your cupboards. Take anything you haven't worn for a year, or used for six months to a charity shop.

Relax in a flotation tank, or if you are strapped for cash, go swimming in your local pool and float about a bit.

Go to an art exhibit, or try a matinee performance at the theatre if you feel self-conscious about going to a show on your own at night.

Look around local churches or museums and galleries. You will be amazed at how little one knows of one's own area and how much you can learn.

Hire a bike, if you don't own one. Many local parks have bikes for hire and you can ride around safely in the park to see if you like it.

Join a book group or start your own by posting an ad in the library.

Create your own website or join an online facility like myspace. Creating your own profile makes you think about who you are and how you would like others to see you. You can often get in touch with old friends and make new ones on line too. Be careful though, put all necessary precautions in place and don't give out your home address.

Go speed dating or join a local pub or bar quiz team.

Start to trace your ancestors on line and create your own family tree.

Or just veg out. It really is up to you. The point is that there are dozens of things you can do if you have the time, and if you are home alone this weekend you do. If you really try to enjoy your time alone you may find that it is addictive. You will also find that you will discover some activities that would be fun to share. Pick up the phone on Sunday evening and invite someone to join you next weekend. Be kind to yourself this weekend, and give yourself a break.

DIVE**Я**SION

Create your own ironic playlist, as a soundtrack to your weekend. Here is just a selection of tracks to dance to, or to cry along with. You choose!

I Will Survive	Gloria Gaynor
Good Day Sunshine	The Beatles
Friends	Bette Midler
Are You Lonesome Tonight?	Elvis Presley
Crying	Roy Orbison
Eleanor Rigby	The Beatles
Dancing Queen	Abba
Saturday Night	Elton John
Sing, Sing, Sing	The Benny Goodman Orchestra
The Laughing Song	Norman Wisdom and Joyce Grenfell

WORDSEARCH: Home alone

```
R  S  L  W  L  I  F  S  V  Z  T  G  M  B  T
E  T  I  N  A  Q  H  A  E  E  Z  O  I  O  N
L  X  U  G  A  L  M  A  L  F  L  U  U  O  R
A  Q  I  G  H  E  K  E  P  P  C  R  Y  K  Z
X  G  L  F  N  T  V  I  N  S  I  M  T  S  S
A  R  S  I  H  I  S  Z  N  S  H  E  N  P  E
T  Z  C  L  S  R  L  E  M  G  H  T  O  K  R
I  S  S  I  E  S  E  C  E  V  R  R  Y  E  U
O  D  O  O  F  E  D  S  Y  I  T  T  R  C  C
N  N  B  Z  O  V  P  M  I  C  N  U  U  V  I
G  N  I  N  E  D  R  A  G  C  C  G  X  S  N
S  W  I  M  M  I  N  G  K  I  R  X  U  M  A
E  R  T  A  E  H  T  F  D  Y  O  E  L  X  M
L  F  P  E  A  C  E  E  C  J  U  E  X  L  A
D  G  D  P  V  N  P  R  D  S  J  R  O  E  Q
```

BOOKS
CINEMA
CYCLING
EXERCISE
FOOD
GARDENING
GOURMET
LUXURY
MANICURE
PEACE
PEDICURE
RELAXATION
SIGHTSEEING
SLEEP
SPA
SPORT
SWIMMING
TELEVISION
THEATRE
TOURISM
WALKING

HANJIE

Shade in squares to reveal a hidden picture. The clue numbers to the top and left reveal how many adjacent shaded squares there are in each column and row respectively. If there are multiple numbers for a row or column then there are multiple sequences of adjacent shaded squares with at least one empty square between them, in the order given. For example, "2, 3" would mean that somewhere in that row or column there are 2 adjacent shaded squares, followed by a gap of one or more squares, followed by 3 adjacent shaded squares.

Hint: It's essential to mark in squares you know to be empty with a dot or cross, otherwise you will find it very hard to solve this puzzle! A good tactic is to start by considering the rows and columns with the most shaded squares.

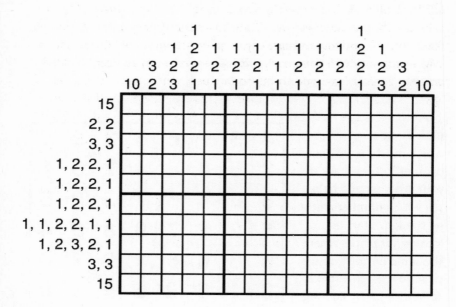

HITORI

Shade in squares so that no number occurs more than once per row or column. Shaded squares cannot touch in either a horizontal or vertical direction. All unshaded squares must form a single continuous area so that you can move from any unshaded square to any other by travelling only horizontally or vertically between them.

Hint: Circle numbers which must be unshaded in order to keep track of your progress and help see which numbers must be shaded. Start by looking for places where the same number occurs close to itself in a row or column, and considering if anything can be deduced from this.

4	5	7	6	8	2	3	2
2	5	4	8	4	7	3	1
8	6	4	6	7	5	2	5
5	2	1	7	6	8	3	4
5	6	8	5	1	2	7	6
3	1	5	2	5	4	1	8
1	6	3	6	2	6	5	6
7	8	1	4	5	1	1	3

SLITHERLINK

Draw a single loop by joining the dots with straight horizontal or vertical lines. Each number specifies how many adjacent dots must be joined in the 'square' around that number. Areas without numbers can have any number of dots joined. The loop cannot touch or cross over itself.

Hint: Start by considering the corners and the 0 and 3 'squares'. Mark the areas between dots that you deduce must not be joined with a small 'x'.

```
.   .   .   .   .   .   .   .   .
      3       3       2   2
.   .   .   .   .   .   .   .   .
  2   2       2       2   2
.   .   .   .   .   .   .   .   .
  2       3           3   3
.   .   .   .   .   .   .   .   .
      2       2               2
.   .   .   .   .   .   .   .   .
  1               1       3
.   .   .   .   .   .   .   .   .
      2   2           1       2
.   .   .   .   .   .   .   .   .
      2   2       1       3   2
.   .   .   .   .   .   .   .   .
      2   3       2       3
.   .   .   .   .   .   .   .   .
```

75

SUDOKU

Place the numbers 1 to 9 into the grid so that each row, column and marked 3x3 box contains each number once and once only.

				6				
	2		3	5	7		1	
	5	7				8	9	
	8		6		9		3	
5								1
	1		2		5		6	
	7	5				3	2	
	9		7	2	1		4	
				3				

Hint: Start by looking for numbers that can fit in only one place in a row, column or 3x3 box.

REBUS PUZZLES

The design of the type and its position in the box gives a clue to its meaning which will be a well known phrase or saying.

TLUASREMOS

.2.

MOD CON MOD CON
MOD CON MOD CON
MOD CON MOD CON
MOD CON MOD CON

LIVE LIVE LIVE LIVE
DAY DAY

EITHER...

'Watch where you are putting your feet' he snarled, as she went into the turn. A furious blush suffused her cheeks, and she was humiliated by the tears that started in her eyes. But Ella was no shrinking Miss. 'Watch where you are putting your hands!' she snapped back. He stalked haughtily from the dance floor, leaving her more crushed than ever. He was an impossible man, but a stunningly good dancer and Ella did not want to lose him as her partner after only three classes. She had always wanted to learn to tango. Her parents, both born and brought up in Argentina, had been world champions. Somehow she had spent her youth avoiding dancing herself. Perhaps she was afraid to compete, to intrude into the intimacy of the dance and their marriage. It was nearly a year since the tragic plane crash that had taken their lives and at last she had taken to the floor. Carlos watched her as she stood under the mirror ball, lost and unhappy, and felt a pang of regret for his behaviour. She was such a promising partner, but she touched his soul in a way that he was unprepared to admit. As the music rose, he sauntered back to take her in his arms once again. He was the picture of arrogance. Suddenly something flashed in Ella's eyes and she lifted her chin defiantly. The other dancers moved to the edge of the floor as she laid the flat of her hand against his chest and pushed him away...

OR...

The handle felt cool in his hands, and he held the blade up to the light. The edge was so sharp it was almost invisible. The knife was his chosen weapon – silent and deadly, and involved. You could not pretend to yourself that you were disconnected from the act when you plunged it deep into another's flesh. He had used this knife for every one of the seven murders. He was not afraid to call it murder. He did not deceive himself. He had cold-bloodedly taken the lives of seven men. He did not call it revenge, or execution, even to himself, though he was certain that it was justice. He knew that the police would look for the murder weapon, but he would not discard it. If they found him, they would find him with his knife in his hand and the victory would be theirs. But they would not find him. There was nothing to connect him to his victims, absolutely nothing. He had chosen them as representatives of their kind, not as individuals and they had nothing in common with one another. He tested the blade against his own flesh and resumed stropping it against the strap held between his wrist and elbow. He was not invincible but he was invisible...

BAD DATE SYNDROME

Everyone seems to be in love, from couples in the park, aged nine to ninety, to F list celebrities in the glossy magazines. But you have been battered by BDS and are thinking of hanging up your dating shoes. Even the cutlery seems to have a better love life than you do, (just look at those naughty spoons, well, spooning!) You have kissed a lot of frogs without a suggestion of 'the artist previously known as' let alone bona-fide royalty appearing. It can be very discouraging to be disappointed time and time again in your quest for the perfect partner, and now you are feeling too low even to make the effort.

When you come to think about it, dating is a very strange way to choose a mate for life, or even just someone to have dinner with. When we meet someone new and arrange a date, nine out of ten of us attack the gym, buy new clothes, try to acquire in-depth knowledge on a whole range of possible subjects to discuss over drinks, and get all done up in our best outfits, and our best personalities to meet our dream man or woman. In short, we re-invent ourselves in the bizarre hope that a total stranger will like this newly minted person, (who we don't even know) better than the one he or she asked out. We invest our new date with all the qualities we most admire too. This is guaranteed to end in tears. Then we find the most socially difficult circumstances we can manage, to test drive our new creation. Let's go out for a meal, before we have discovered if our date is a vegetarian, a gourmet or a burger addict. Let's arrange to see a movie before we've found out what kind of films he or she likes, or maybe arrange to meet in a noisy club or at a party where we can't hear what the other is saying (all that studying topics of conversation for nought) and so on. In short, we set ourselves up to have a tricky time and with each passing date, our confidence dwindles, and we start making those lists about why a hat is better than a man, or a coal scuttle is easier to live with than a woman.

Also 'they' *seem* to change the rules every so often and if you have been out of the game for a while, it is easy to blunder into a minefield of social gaffes. No wonder that so many of us get depressed about dating. It's time to calm down and draw the line under unrealistic expectations. But while you wait for your nails to dry or, with pounding heart, for your dream date to pick you up for the prom, divert yourself, by sharpening your wits with the puzzles that follow. The knees may be weak but the brain is willing.

HOT TIPS

Never make or accept a marriage proposal on a first date.

Always tell someone where you are going and organise a pre-arranged phone signal with a friend in case you need rescuing from a date.

Never arrange to meet outside a venue or in a dark and dingy bar. Offer to pick up your date, or arrange for him or her to pick you up. This is not because all first dates are potential maniacs, fiends or bunny-boilers, but because it is so humiliating and depressing to be stood up in a public place.

If you are going out to eat, discuss what kind of cuisine you like, before you go. A few text enquires will do. It can avoid hours of misery trying to force down something you hate.

Do not change your appearance radically between arranging the date and the date itself. Apart from the fact that you might not recognise one another if you have foolishly ignored tip three, it is a mistake to start out trying to be something you are not. That is not to say we don't all want to look our best, of course we do, but don't go for sexy siren if you are more comfortable as Miss Daisy, or Sophisticated International Man of Mystery if you are really the boy next door. Be your best self, but be yourself!

Remember this is a date, not a test. It is supposed to be fun, a chance to spend entertaining time together to see if you like one another. You don't fail dates, any more than you fail relationships or fail marriage. Thinking in those terms just diminishes your confidence. In fact, I wish someone would ban that sort of terminology when it comes to human relationships. Discovering what you don't have in common is as important as being totally compatible. You will recognise the signs more quickly next time. Look on dating as a learning experience. Also, you may be looking for a life partner, but if you give dating a proper chance you might find a new friend rather than a lover. Friends have friends and you have more chance of meeting new people through friends than hanging out in singles bars.

Go out to have the best time you can, and more importantly to make your date feel comfortable and ensure that you both have a good time. The journey, as the wise man said, is as important as getting there.

Listen to your date. We are often so keen to show how interesting and clever we are that we never discover how interesting and clever the other person is.

Choose an imaginative first date. Tea at a swanky hotel for example, or a trip to the zoo or the circus, rather than the standard and often loaded 'dinner'.

Expect to pay your share and always have enough cash for a cab, if the going gets tough.

If it turns out to be another lousy date, put it down to experience and dust off your dating shoes before taking them for another spin.

DIVEЯSION

Would like to meet

Write an honest personal ad for yourself, as if you were going to place it in a 'lonely hearts' column. Then write the ideal ad for your dream partner. You must imagine that you are paying for this by the word, so be succinct. Use no more than 20 words for each ad.

First you have to learn the lingo. Answers to these acronyms are given at the back of the book.

GSOH	**OIOH**	**GFAW**	**FVF**
GM/GW	**OHAT**	**LAF**	**BAV**
NB	**OG/OB**	**TDAH**	**KIR**

WORDSEARCH: Bad date syndrome

```
O T P E R E A O L D L L M F E
O N C E S U R Q R N A Q O L N
L G U N R E O I Z N L U V O I
D S E F L F V M O J S F I W T
G S Z A X E E S U K V I E E N
S C X D B K R C S H U U G R E
E E K B Q E W G T V J R A S L
D J T O P S S I M A Q U P C A
R X X A P I H S D N E I R F V
E Y H Y L H R W F P O Z Q E L
N V Z W P O G N I D D E W C L
N B N R O D C R O M A N T I C
I R I G H T D O R M X T S O D
D L U N A I N L H E T B E N A
H Q S A O A D H L C L R J S J
```

CHOCOLATES
DATES
DINNER
DRIVE
FLOWERS
FRIENDSHIP
FUN
MISS/MR/RIGHT
MOVIE
PERFECT
PERSONAL
RELAXED
ROMANTIC
SENSE/OF/HUMOUR
VALENTINE
WEDDING

HITORI

Shade in squares so that no number occurs more than once per row or column. Shaded squares cannot touch in either a horizontal or vertical direction. All unshaded squares must form a single continuous area so that you can move from any unshaded square to any other by travelling only horizontally or vertically between them.

Hint: Circle numbers which must be unshaded in order to keep track of your progress and help see which numbers must be shaded. Start by looking for places where the same number occurs close to itself in a row or column, and considering if anything can be deduced from this.

1	2	4	7	8	7	3	7
8	7	6	5	6	1	2	8
6	4	3	7	2	4	1	8
8	1	5	3	5	2	2	6
3	4	8	4	7	7	6	1
7	8	1	6	3	5	4	8
4	7	7	7	1	3	4	2
7	3	1	2	6	8	7	4

KAKURO

Place only the numbers 1 to 9 into the empty white squares so that each across or down run of white squares adds up to the total above or to the left of it. No number can be used more than once in any run, so you cannot use 2 and 2 to add up to '4'. Numbers to the right of the diagonal line give the sum of squares to the right; numbers below the diagonal line give the sum of squares below.

Hint: Start by looking for runs of white squares where only one set of digits will fit, such as 16 (7 and 9) or 17 (8 and 9).

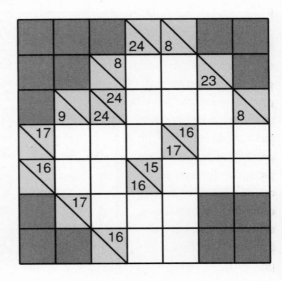

88

IRREGULAR SUDOKU

Place the numbers 1 to 9 into the grid so that each row, column and bold shape contains each number once and once only.

Hint: You can sometimes use the widest part of each shape, and the way in which it overlaps with a row or column, to help eliminate possibilities.

	3			2			9	
7								6
	2						3	
		3				5		
9				4				5
		7				8		
	8						1	
1								9
	1			7			6	

IRREGULAR SUDOKU

Place the numbers 1 to 9 into the grid so that each row, column and bold shape contains each number once and once only.

Hint: You can sometimes use the widest part of each shape, and the way in which it overlaps with a row or column, to help eliminate possibilities.

9				5				2
		4				9		
1	7						9	6
		1				5		
6	8						5	4
		2				1		
3				4				9

DIVERSION

What are these stick people saying to one another?

What is wrong with this alphabet?

A
B
C
D
E
F
G
H
I
J
K
L
M
N
O
P
Q
R
S
T
U
V
W
X
Y
Z

SOCIAL DILEMMAS

These are lateral thinking problems, rather than literal ones, so you need to approach them from a fresh angle.

Switched on

You get back to your date's home and ask to use the bathroom. It is an interior room with no windows and there are three light switches on the outside. For some reason you must know which switch lights which lightbulb, and you can only go into the room once. How can you tell?

The tyres they are a-changing

Your date is driving you home when the car gets a flat tyre. You both get out to replace it with the spare. It is dark and rainy and you are parked on a hill. He removes the four wheel nuts and places them on the ground. Unfortunately, they roll down the gutter and into a deep storm drain and are lost forever. You have the solution to his problem and it means you will both get home in the car instead of having to stay in Bates' Motel nearby. What is it?

REBUS PUZZLES

The design of the type and its position in the box gives a clue to its meaning which will be a well known phrase or saying.

**DNUORG
WORK**

PRAY **RAIN
RAIN
RAIN
RAIN**

OCEDROPAN

**S   N
U   U
N   S**

ADOLESCENCE: IT'S PMS

Tantrums and tears, door slamming, grunts, self-consciousness, keeping vampire hours and a desperate need for independence and privacy – all perfectly normal behaviour – and that's just the parents. But if you are between 10 and 22 your hormones are raging as well, your bodies are changing and no one seems to understand you anymore. PMS usually stands for pre-menstrual syndrome, something many adolescent girls suffer from when they reach puberty, which can lead to emotional outbursts, mood swings and even aggressive behaviour. But at least we all know what is causing it, and we can take Evening Primrose oil and other herbal supplements that may help. In my book, it also stands for Pre-Maturity Syndrome, a condition that affects young men and women (and a few Peter Pan types I know) equally, though in different ways.

Research has now found that this is not just a period of anti-social behaviour associated with needing to reject the values of the previous generation. In fact, it is something which young people cannot avoid to some degree, because their brains do not fully mature until their early twenties, whilst their bodies are being assaulted by changes more comprehensive than at any other time in their lives, except perhaps in their mothers' wombs. No, this is not a licence to behave badly, but it is worth knowing about, for both parents and adolescents.

At this time, so-called teens are under enormous social pressure, from their peers, from their teachers and from their parents. It is no wonder that many of them do not wake up in the morning, bright-eyed and bushy-tailed and looking forward to a brand new day. Mind you, neither do their parents! 'So it's normal then,' I hear you say. Well, yes it is normal but that doesn't mean that parents and young people can't make it easier for one another. If you are a parent, please try to be patient and supportive and preserve sensible boundaries that will keep your young person safe and feeling secure, no matter how hard they fight against it. But make your few basic home rules simple, fair, understanding and understandable. They will forget things from time to time, that's part of this brain development thing.

If you are an adolescent, please remember that courtesy of some awful cosmic joke, your parents are probably also going through Middlescence, (see page 123) and their hormones are also up the creek, especially your Mum's. They are also probably about as financially stretched as they can be, and they are in the ideal position to look back on their own youth and regret missed opportunities. But they do love you, and you can try to find a way to help them to help you grow up, without hurting one another too much. Sorry if this bit sounds rather obvious, it's just that sometimes, someone needs to say 'give each other a break.' Teen angst can become more serious and lead to depression and that is something everyone wants to avoid. Solving problems, however silly can help the vital cognitive functions of your brain to develop, and help relieve some of the symptoms that can make you feel so wretched. They also pass the time, which seems to hang so heavy on your hands while you are waiting to start your real life as an adult. If you are an adult, they can help to keep your synapses firing and give you some breathing space to take stock and regroup and other clichés. So have a go at some of the diversions in this book. In the meantime, please bear with the good advice below.

HOT TIPS

Laugh as loudly and as often as possible, but make sure you are laughing with people, not at them.

Try to get enough sleep to sustain your growth – in bed that is, not in school. Try going to bed an hour earlier than usual at least one night in three.

Get some physical exercise, even if it is riding a bike or walking to school or work, or dancing. Not only does this improve your fitness and stamina, and help you to that body to die for, fresh air can also help skin problems and the exercise releases endorphins, which will help you feel calmer and more relaxed and help with those mood swings.

Do the relaxation and deep breathing exercises on pages 12-16 when stress makes it difficult to sleep or to concentrate, around exam time, for example.

Eat plenty of fresh fruit and vegetables. Boring maybe, but once again they will help with spots, help you to healthy weight control and make you feel better able to cope.

Drink plenty of water, at least two litres a day. Skin again, the water helps clear toxins from the system.

Avoid excessive booze; I know it can make you feel more confident and less inhibited at first, but it can literally be soul destroying to have forgotten huge chunks of your night, if not your youth. The embarrassment and humiliation of throwing up on your shoes, or worse, waking up feeling like death and possibly with someone whose name you don't know, and who doesn't know yours, and cares even less, can be devastating. Drugs will do that too of course. It's true that you may be one of the lucky ones for whom there are no physical or psychological dire consequences to binge drinking, or recreational drugs, but how will you know until it is too late?

Try not to give into peer pressure to do anything, which makes you feel uncomfortable. Easier said than done I know, but though you might hope the crowd of which you want to be a part will like you better, you could find you like yourself less, and that will bring you down. It is bad enough to feel that your life is controlled by everyone else, parents, teachers, everyone. So why give control to your peers as well?

DON'T start smoking. Don't give nicotine control over you either.

Take care of this great new body. I know it's like being given a new computer and then being told not to take it out of the carton and try it out. But go easy, early sexual activity isn't for everyone and unhappy sex is very far from the joyous experience you have a right to expect. If you do want to have sex, use protection, and make sure you both demand and give the love and respect you deserve.

DO not put up with being bullied physically or emotionally, tell someone older, who you can trust. This needn't be a teacher or parent, but it needs to be someone who can help you deal with the problem in a way that makes you comfortable and happy. But dealt with it must be, and you need to accept that you may need help.

Think about the coolest people you know. The essence of coolness is to be your own person, not one of a crowd. That doesn't mean you can't like the same fashion and music as your mates; finding out what we have in common with one another is what makes us socialised human beings, but if you have different tastes or views, don't be afraid to express them.

Love yourself. I know you hate your legs, or your nose or your feet or some other part of your body. I know you feel stupid and inadequate and unloved or unlovable, but remember your teen feels just the same. Until you like yourself, you are giving off the wrong signals. You can't expect other people to like you.

Wear Sunscreen.

WORSEARCH: Adolescence

```
T Z K N O I H S A F G V B W A
M N I V C E E C H A N G E P G
U J E X E N F O M L L H D D O
S Q E M O S N E E T I R A O Y
I B W M E Q S G K U H N B S T
C S R S Z T W L A D C O Y A I
A O P I C Y I A O I U G P U S
H O R S I H O C N O R S F U N
E Z I P T N O G X E C E W H E
J C V Q X N T O N E Q H E E T
C S A T E E E E L M B T N O N
M L C T A S H R R D M O S L I
J C Y F W G X R A N L L F G B
Y T I R A L U P O P E C C D B
S H O P P I N G D N T T S Y A
```

CHANGE
CLOTHES
COOL
DANCING
ENERGY
EXCITEMENT
FASHION
GAMES
HORMONES
INTENSITY
INTERNET
MUSIC
NEW
PARENTS
POPULARITY
PRIVACY
SCHOOL
SHOPPING
TEENS

URGR8

Text messages to send to friends or even your parents to make them feel good. Answers at the back of the book.

BETBstUCnBE	**EvrEDAInEvrEWAURGttnBTa&BTa**
ULkGR8	**HlMmImSAf**
ShnOnSpaS*	**UcnDoIt**
ILuvU	**DntWrEBHaPE**
URBUtifl	**NvaSANva**

SUDOKU

Place the numbers 1 to 9 into the grid so that each row, column and marked 3x3 box contains each number once and once only.

1		4				6		9
	5		4		7		3	
		3		2		4		
			2	9	4			
				8				
			1	3	6			
		6		7		9		
	3		5		9		1	
5		9				8		2

Hint: Start by looking for numbers that can fit in only one place in a row, column or 3x3 box.

103

SLITHERLINK

Draw a single loop by joining the dots with straight horizontal or vertical lines. Each number specifies how many adjacent dots must be joined in the 'square' around that number. Areas without numbers can have any number of dots joined. The loop cannot touch or cross over itself.

Hint: Start by considering the corners and the 0 and 3 'squares'. Mark the areas between dots that you deduce must not be joined with a small 'x'.

```
   2     2     3     1     3
   2     3     2     0     2
3    2     1     1  2     1
   2  2  3  2  2  3     2  3
3  2     1  1  1  2  2  2
2     3  1     2     2     3
2     2     3     2     1
2     3     2     2     1
```

KAKURO

DIVE:RSION

Place only the numbers 1 to 9 into the empty white squares so that each across or down run of white squares adds up to the total above or to the left of it. No number can be used more than once in any run, so you cannot use 2 and 2 to add up to '4'. Numbers to the right of the diagonal line give the sum of squares to the right; numbers below the diagonal line give the sum of squares below.

Hint: Start by looking for runs of white squares where only one set of digits will fit, such as 16 (7 and 9) or 17 (8 and 9).

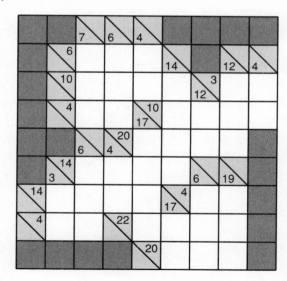

HANJIE

Shade in squares to reveal a hidden picture. The clue numbers to the top and left reveal how many adjacent shaded squares there are in each column and row respectively. If there are multiple numbers for a row or column then there are multiple sequences of adjacent shaded squares with at least one empty square between them, in the order given. For example, "2, 3" would mean that somewhere in that row or column there are 2 adjacent shaded squares, followed by a gap of one or more squares, followed by 3 adjacent shaded squares.

Hint: It's essential to mark in squares you know to be empty with a dot or cross, otherwise you will find it very hard to solve this puzzle! A good tactic is to start by considering the rows and columns with the most shaded squares.

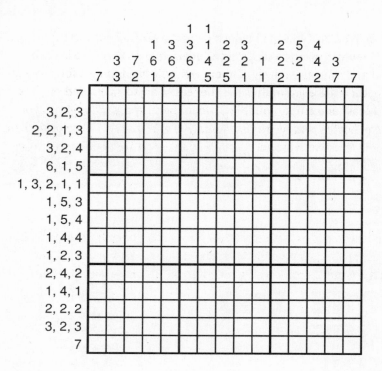

The design of the type and its position in the box gives a clue to its meaning which will be a well known phrase or saying.

EVER
EVER
EVER
EVER

IDEA

GONE
GONE   **END**
GONE
GONE

NA
UN
RD

SOUNDTRACK OF YOUR LIFE

Create a playlist of songs that suit your mood
Here are some examples to start you off.

Young Americans	David Bowie
Young Guns (go for it)	Wham
Young Soul Rebels	Mica Paris
The Young Ones	Cliff Richard and The Shadows
Young Hearts Run Free	Candi Staton
The Young MC	Superfunk
Young Gifted and Black	Bob and Marcia
Young Turks	Rod Stewart
Young Parisians	Adam and the Ants
Young Girl	Gary Puckett and the Union Gap

Write a short story

(2000 words) It should begin

EITHER...

14th November

Dad was just so embarrassing tonight. No-one else's dad insists on driving his daughter to parties AND picking her up. When Floyd turned on the lights and said in his most mocking voice, 'Anna Jansen, your father's here, 'I could have died.

He might as well have come out in his pyjamas; he looked so uncool (Dad, not Floyd, he is just amazingly cool) with his hair all stuck up on end and his sweat- shirt over his shirt and tie. It even has a hood! He looked like, half asleep All the way home Dad kept asking if I'd had a nice time, and what did I eat and stuff, as if I'd been to a kid's birthday party, like I was five or something. Just said 'Whatever'. I know it drives him mad. Texted Sara (or Zarah as she now calls herself) to find out if Floyd had got off with anyone else after I left. She didn't answer which probably means she got off with him. Her mum doesn't make her leave parties just as they are getting hot. I so hate her (Mum that is, not Zarah, although I don't know!) Got home and Mum kept sniffing me for like booze or something. Bet Floyd walks Zarah home, she will definitely kiss him. I thought he was going to snog me at the party even though I have a zit on my chin that I tried to cover with concealer, and then the doorbell rang. I don't know if he really likes me, he always kisses someone at parties. Zarah says she would do it with him if he asks her. I will probably die a virgin. I HATE my life...

OR...

His breath was ragged now as he powered up the incline. Nothing in the training manual had prepared him for this. The months at boot camp seemed like a picnic compared with the past week. The leaders were far ahead of him now, while the losers were so far behind that he could imagine himself to be totally alone. He paused to catch his breath and drink a little of his precious water. He knew he should conserve it, and who knew when he would find a fresh supply, in this perpetual darkness. If he only he not dropped the light map he might have a chance. As it was he had relied upon what the mentors had described as instinct. This power had not been used in living memory and he had worked hard to develop a rudimentary skill in auditory noticing. Visual lightening would not be much help to him in the thickness of the dark, but the lingual bud teasing and nasal recognition had saved him from poisoning when his feeder tube had ruptured, and he had been forced to forage for nourishment.

Now he tried to recall the fifth lesson, extended digital exploration. His digits were frail, but the exercises were beginning to pay off and using them to 'feel' his way along the precipitous path might be his only hope of survival. He tried breathing again and this time the air seemed to fill his tiny lungs with oxygen. He was even beginning to imagine a landscape beyond the sharpness of his world. Perhaps that landscape would be many-hued but how would he distinguish between the shades? How would he know what to call them without a companion with whom to share the naming? He began to whimper as he contemplated the rest of his journey without a presence to accompany him...

MYSTERY IN THE MIDDLE

This little mystery is for you to solve any time you have to battle boredom or gloom. Good luck! The solution can be found at the back of the book.

The following is a record of the email correspondence between two friends, one in England, the other in New York, about the curious messages received by Sir Orphington-Sprogg. Guy and Stacy achieved some fame when they solved a murder email mystery in Paris. Now Sir Orphington has a problem of his own. Can you solve the mystery contained in the messages he has received? Guy And Stacy's correspondence contains clues, but the hidden messages are contained within the emails he received. The final solution can be found at the back of the book.

From Stacy Michaels
To Guy Barton
cc
Subject: Here we go again

Hi Guy,
Well, I guess we are famous. Ever since the Jean-Luc Cordova mystery,
I have been receiving emails asking me to crack codes. This one looks
interesting though. Have you heard of Sir Orphington-Sprogg, billionaire
philanthropist? He lives in a castle in Cornwall. I am a bit of a fan actually,
because he supports one of my favourite charities.

Anyway it would seem that, every time he logs on to his personal email
he gets a message like the one attached. Of course he gets dozens of
requests for donations, but these are thank you letters for donations he
hasn't made.

Let me know if you think we can help.
Love Stacy

From Dotherboys Ophanage
To Sir Orphington Sprogg
Cc
Subject Your kindness

Dear Sir Orphington

I am Writing to tHank you on bE half of the childREn at our
orphAnage for youR most gEnerous donation.

The opportuNities that will now be available to some of the
most disadvantaged children in England are beyond oUr and Their
expectations. We are intending to take the most deserving on a
tour of the local mines in your honour.

Your KINdnesS is WIlDly inspiring giving hOpe to those Who
have been abandoned. One of our lads is hoping to become an
engineer and your donations will help fund his education.

PleAse kNow your Dedicated and Caring Help Is LauDable and
an inspiration to us all.

Yours very sincerely,
Cyril Rodente

From Guy Barton
To Stacy Michaels
Cc
Subject Re Here we go again

Hi Stacy,
You English are very strange, why would anyone call an orphanage after
Dickens' terrible school? Still that is not all that is strange! Looks like this
may indeed be coded. I hadn't heard of Sir Orph, but I googled him and I
was really interested to find that he made his pile in Canada in the 60s.
Do you remember he opened up an old gold mine on the advice of his
partner, an engineer called Jim Nutkin and struck it rich? Please send me
the other messages.
Guy

From Stacy Michaels
To Guy Barton
cc
Subject: Poor Sir Orphington.

Hi Guy,

I attach the next curious email which Sir Orphington has received. Check out the charity this time. I know we British are eccentric but surely this is just a joke? Do you have badgers in the States? He seems strangely upset by getting these. I checked out that gold strike in the 60s. You are right, he was just another businessman of average means before then. What happened to Nutkin I wonder? There seems to be no mention of him in the official records of Sir Orphington's companies.

Good luck with the code.
Stacy

From The Healthy Badger Society
To Sir Orphington Sprogg
Cc
Subject The badgers thank you

Dear Sir Orphington,
Many thaks for yor splendid donation to the Healhy Badger
Society. It is a little nown charty but a important one.

Did you kow that four thousand badgers die needlessly every
year due to tuberculosis? Farmers do not keep their cattle
adequately vaccinated and this in turn causes the disease to
spread to the badger populations. Ho is this possible with
tody's modern medicine and facilitie? It is because the
average person does not understand the importance and
contribution of badgers to the baance of nature and the
environmnt.

It is vital that the HBS inorms the general public of this
situaion. Publiciy for this nble cause will ensure that all
bagers are protected now and n the forseable future.
Thank you again for your most valuable donation.

Your obedient servant,
Miss Loretta Plumley

From Guy Barton
To Stacy Michaels
Cc
Subject Of course we have badgers

Hi Stacy,

Of course we have badgers, it's not all bears and groundhogs here you know. I am getting worried by the tone of these messages though. Have you cracked the code? It seems someone else is asking questions. Please send me the next message urgently. We need to find whoever is sending them.There is no mention of Jim Nutkin in any of the accounts of the gold strike after the first news of their find. Could be there's a connection?

Guy

From Stacy Michaels
To Guy Barton
cc
Subject: Curiouser and curiouser

Hi Guy,
Take a look at these. At first Sir Orphington thought the first was
genuine, but then he noticed the typing errors. The sender is clever
though, these use different codes again. I am beginning to be seriously
anxious and so is Sir Orphington. We had better get a move on here.
Bognor Regis is a small seaside resort on the south coast of England by
the way.
Love
Stacy

**From The Blue Ribbon Charity- to find a cure
for prostate cancer
To Sir Orphington Sprogg
Cc
Subject You have made such a difference**

Dear Sir Orphington

The Blue Ribbon Charity can not thank you enough for the
donation of the wonderful research facilities. Dr Crippen was
particularly excited, so much so hu immediately sent for
details of specialist equipment.

It as our intention to name the new unit in your honour and
hope that you will net find this presumptuous. You are well
known for your modesty when giving such large endowments which
is of course very commendable. However we would like to take
advantage of using your name to encourage awareness of the
illness, both to attract more donations but also to encourage
men to have regular check ups.

Prostate cancer is a very serious killer. Many men are unaware
of how easy and painless it is to have routine checks. When
prostate cancer is caught early there is a very high success
rate in making a full recovery.

Your generosity will not be fergettun.
Very sincerely yours,
Argylle McCloud

121

From Single Mums Stranded in Bognor Appeal
To Sir Orphington Sprogg
Cc
Subject You give us hope

Dear Sir Ophington,

You darling man you have come to the rescue of the most deserving single mothers. We are a small and very new charity so it is a tremendous surprise that you have heard of us and are willing to provide us with financial support.

I cannot tell you the distress our single mums feel when after birth to their innocent babes, these young girls (and not so young) discover that they are trapped forever in Bognor. The desperation of knowing there is
nowhere else to go and no real future to look forward to is enough to drive them to drink.

Your donation provides us with the needed ponec to send several of these single girls for a week's break in Brighton. This fiqq no doubt inspire them to retrain as hairdressers and noh just sit at home all day. With these new skills these mums can dream of leaving Bognor and moving to exotic places such as Bournemouth.

We at SMSiBA all think that you are a knight in shining armour
here to jage us. Cou will always be in our thoughts.

Lots of luv,

Bev

From Guy Barton
To Stacy Michaels
Cc
Subject Urgent

Stacy,

This is getting beyond a joke. Get in touch with the police and ask them
to give Sir Orphington round the clock protection.

Guy

From Stacy Michaels
To Guy Barton
cc
Subject: It's too late

Guy,

It's so awful, Sir Orphington-Sprogg was found dead this morning.
It seems he was trying to find a rare bottle of vintage wine in his cellar,
when a rack of wine bottles collapsed on him, trapping him beneath.
He had just sent me this latest email, which I have cracked and I have
passed the whole matter on to the police. They suspect foul play!
We must help them track down the sender.

Stacy

From Society for Environmentally Friendly Interments
To Sir Orphington Sprogg
Cc
Subject When it's time to go

Dear Sir Ophington,

How gratifying It is to know that someone of your eminence
supporTs environmentally friendly IntermentS. Just think what
damage is being done to the environment by Yellow brass knObbed
caskets and smoking crematoria! Imagine the destrUction of
haRdwood Trees to make coffins that are seen for an hoUr or two
and then buRied!! ANd all This waste fOr nothing but
affectation.

How much nicer to be placed in a pasteboard simulateD wooden box
and tucked neatly Into the ground under a sweet chEstnut tree.

The Society for Environmentally Friendly Interments will use
your kind and generous contribution to run a publicity campaign
making everyone aware that their death can help feed the earth
and not poison it.

Thank you again for your wonderful donation.

Yours truly,

Obadiah Smythe.

MIDDLESCENCE: IT'S HRT

HRT, as every woman over forty will know, stands for hormone replacement therapy; the balanced combination of hormones which, if properly prescribed and monitored, can transform the lives of women during the menopause. HRT can indeed relieve the symptoms from hell (the burning hot flashes, night sweats and mood swings are the very devil) but don't think that this chapter doesn't apply to you if you are of the male persuasion. In this book HRT also stands for happiness ratio theory. This is the theory, that in our 21st century, youth -obsessed world, your happiness will decrease in direct proportion to your age as soon as you blow out the candles on your fortieth birthday cake.

You haven't felt this confused since you were a teenager. One day you feel on top of the world, proud of your achievements, and free for the first time for years from some of your responsibilities. Just for the moment, there is a brief respite in the struggle of getting and spending and competing and raising children. Sadly, the next day your hormones gang up on you and your world tilts vertiginously. You battle with the earth's gravitational pull on your assets and realise and that the expensive potions are no longer 'reducing the appearance of wrinkles' (that word 'appearance' is a giveaway isn't it? The wrinkles are still there, but you notice them less through the rose-tinted spectacles that came with the pot of snake oil.) You can't remember where you put the spectacles you didn't need yesterday.

You are working now to support a bevy of stylists and therapists who rush at you with hair colouring, botox, collagen and as many cosmetic procedures as your blood pressure and your bank balance will allow. If you are a man, you may be clinging on to the tossing golden curls, which seem to be slipping off your head like a duvet in the night, and regarding your 'pecs' and 'abs' and other abbreviations for bodily parts with some dismay. You may even be starting to *read* the junk mail we are all plagued with, offering performance enhancing drugs and various enlargements. Whatever your gender, you feel you should no longer eat anything you enjoy, and the competitive exercise wear at the gym is getting you down. Maintaining the 'you' in youth is a full time commitment from forty to seventy and beyond. Don't you know, shout the newspaper and magazine headlines, that grey is the new black and fifty is the new thirty?

You know, you can be happier as a 'middlescent' than at any other time in your life, but it takes really positive and decisive thinking to pull it off. The power of the grey pound or dollar has never been stronger. Enjoying middle age just takes practice and a real change of attitude. Keep the synapses in your brain firing, and everything else will follow. Your mind and your memory need an aerobic work out every day, so divert yourself with as many puzzles and games as you can. You are still you, even if your mother or father now peers back at you from the bathroom mirror each day. Be true to yourself.

HOT TIPS

'Be nice to your children, they will be choosing your rest home later on.'

Enjoy your achievements and the benefit of your experience. You have every right to be proud of yourself.

It is never too late to change your career, or embrace a new phase in life. Don't fear change, it can be good as well as bad, and we human beings are designed to solve the problems it brings.

Make sensible provision for the future, just as you always have, but don't circumscribe your enjoyment of life now to do it.

Don't worry constantly about your health, but do have regular health checks, especially for your blood pressure, hormone imbalances, cholesterol and late onset diabetes

Take regular exercise in the fresh air. No Spandex required. Walking briskly, cycling, swimming and dancing are all good for your heart and your joints. But if you enjoy free-fall parachuting and off-piste skiing, don't give them up!

Enjoy a healthy, balanced diet with plenty of fresh fruit and vegetables, at least five a day, and don't eat red meat more than once or twice a week. Cut down on salt, saturated fats and refined sugar. Eat oily fish at least twice a week or take good quality Omega 3 fish oil supplements. Try to include unsalted nuts and red berries in your diet.

That being said, treat yourself to lunch or dinner out with friends, at a really great restaurant, at least once a month, and don't deprive yourself of everything you enjoy. Reward yourself with the occasional high calorie dessert.

Use this rule of thumb, glass of fine wine with dinner – good, three martinis before lunch – bad!

Enjoy the company of the young; they have fresh notions that challenge your thinking and stop you becoming entrenched in old ideas.

Do at least one thing a week that boosts your self-confidence. Do have your hair styled and cut well, and coloured too, if it makes you feel good. Have a manicure or a facial because you really are worth it.

Look after your feet; they have a lot to put up with. Get a pedicure once a month.

Have a really good massage once a week.

Book a weekend away in a foreign country as a reward for learning the language. Give yourself six weeks to master basic everyday conversation.

De-clutter your wardrobe and your home. Hold onto really important mementos, but take any clothes in to which you can only just squeeze and have had for ten years or more to the thrift shop.

Treat yourself to new clothes. Book a personal shopper to help you choose, especially if you feel you have got stuck in a particular look for some time.

Update your CV or resumé. Go online to see how. Then apply for a new job, if you feel in a rut at work.

Make love as often as possible.

Laugh as often as possible, not necessarily at the same time as making love.

Volunteer to help the community in some way. You have enough experience of life now to be able to give others the benefit of it.

Check your work life balance. Can you afford to ease up a little on the high achieving and enjoy some down time?

Move house if you feel you would be happier in another location. Yes, your children, if you have them, may well expect you to stay in the family home until you die, But if you think you would be happier by the ocean or in Paris or Mexico, move. They will still visit you and you can always visit them. If you decide to stay put, are there changes you would like to make, redecorating or remodelling for example?

Don't be afraid to meet new people, learn new skills or follow new interests.

Don't indulge in regrets for past mistakes. Move on and make some new ones.

Get plenty of rest, living this new life as the new you can be exhausting.

KAKURO

Place only the numbers 1 to 9 into the empty white squares so that each across or down run of white squares adds up to the total above or to the left of it. No number can be used more than once in any run, so you cannot use 2 and 2 to add up to '4'. Numbers to the right of the diagonal line give the sum of squares to the right; numbers below the diagonal line give the sum of squares below.

Hint: Start by looking for runs of white squares where only one set of digits will fit, such as 16 (7 and 9) or 17 (8 and 9).

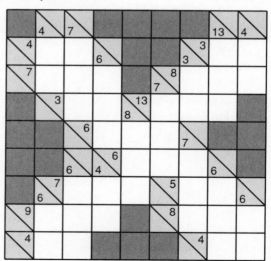

133

HANJIE

Shade in squares to reveal a hidden picture. The clue numbers to the top and left reveal how many adjacent shaded squares there are in each column and row respectively. If there are multiple numbers for a row or column then there are multiple sequences of adjacent shaded squares with at least one empty square between them, in the order given. For example, "2, 3" would mean that somewhere in that row or column there are 2 adjacent shaded squares, followed by a gap of one or more squares, followed by 3 adjacent shaded squares.

Hint: It's essential to mark in squares you know to be empty with a dot or cross, otherwise you will find it very hard to solve this puzzle! A good tactic is to start by considering the rows and columns with the most shaded squares.

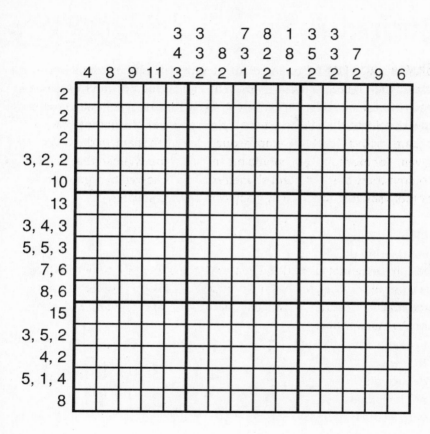

SLITHERLINK

Draw a single loop by joining the dots with straight horizontal or vertical lines. Each number specifies how many adjacent dots must be joined in the 'square' around that number. Areas without numbers can have any number of dots joined. The loop cannot touch or cross over itself.

Hint: Start by considering the corners and the 0 and 3 'squares'. Mark the areas between dots that you deduce must not be joined with a small 'x'.

```
        1     2 2     1 0
   2     0     2     2     1
   3 1     1     2 3     1 3
       0     2     2     0
         1     1     1     0
   2 1     1 2     0     0 1
       3     2     3     0     1
       2 2     1 3       1
```

IRREGULAR SUDOKU

Place the numbers 1 to 9 into the grid so that each row, column and bold shape contains each number once and once only.

Hint: You can sometimes use the widest part of each shape, and the way in which it overlaps with a row or column, to help eliminate possibilities.

				9		5		
3	8			7			5	6
		7				3		
			6		3			
		4				2		
2	9			5			8	1
			8		9			

WORDSEARCH: Middlescence

```
R  P  B  R  V  E  P  W  D  A  O  Y  M  Q  W
E  E  L  S  Z  X  Z  B  H  A  I  R  C  U  T
S  N  L  I  W  P  J  A  G  X  I  O  J  B  Y
I  S  V  A  Q  E  K  S  B  D  S  V  N  O  Z
C  I  C  I  T  R  N  N  S  M  S  C  H  T  J
R  O  F  O  N  I  I  S  E  N  O  M  R  O  H
E  N  Q  L  M  E  O  T  P  G  F  F  C  X  X
X  L  H  A  L  N  I  N  R  O  A  F  P  L  B
E  S  T  E  P  C  K  E  S  S  T  L  U  R  M
G  I  L  R  S  E  E  H  H  H  T  I  L  M  H
V  N  A  V  A  R  X  I  E  N  I  N  O  O  A
D  L  E  A  A  V  O  U  J  K  C  P  I  N  C
U  C  H  C  V  N  E  Z  I  A  T  F  S  O  S
E  R  U  S  I  E  L  L  S  A  V  O  E  J  J
F  A  M  I  L  Y  I  H  R  E  K  E  J  P  X
```

BOTOX
CAREER
CASH
COLLAGEN
COSMETICS
EXERCISE
EXPERIENCE
FAMILY
FASHION
HAIRCUT
HEALTH
HORMONES
JOINTS
LEISURE
PENSION
PETS
POTIONS
RELATIONSHIPS
TRAVEL
VITAMINS

CONFUSION

These are lateral thinking problems, perfect mental aerobics for a middlescent. Approach them from a different angle, not logical linear thinking.

Emergency: A father is driving his son back to university, when a car pulls out from nowhere and ploughs into them. The father is uninjured but his son is badly hurt. Dad calls an ambulance and the son is rushed to hospital for emergency surgery. The surgeon looks at him and says "I can't operate on him, he's my son". Explain.

Bankrupt: A man is seen pushing a car. He looks hot and bothered, but that doesn't explain why, when he finally stops at a hotel, he bursts into tears and tears his hair out.

ASBO: A man has recently escaped from prison and is making his way home on foot. He is walking along a straight, country lane in broad daylight. He has got about two miles from the prison, when he sees a police car coming toward him. Despite knowing that all squads would be out looking for him, he runs towards the car for a short while, and only when he is about ten feet away, does he turn and run into the woods to hide. Why does he run towards the police car?

REBUS PUZZLES

The design of the type and its position in the box gives a clue to its meaning which will be a well known phrase or saying.

MIND
MATTER

OUT LUNCH
LUNCH
LUNCH
LUNCH

TRANSLOSTATION

EMPTY NEST/FULL NEST SYNDROME

It's a tough life, being Mrs Blackbird. She finds a mate, they build a nest together, he hops off, she gives up her promising singing career to stay at home and hatch her eggs, and then spends every day flying back and forth popping delicacies into the ever-open mouths of her hungry, demanding chicks. She feeds and protects them until they are big enough to fend for themselves, worrying her little head about their futures, and the nest is getting pretty cramped. Then suddenly, one day, her work is done, they just spread their wings and fly away. Her slightly battered nest seems very empty indeed. They never phone; they never write, but at least she's still young enough to take up that recording contract, and she doesn't have to do laundry. I expect there is a bit of nest work, but certainly no parents' conferences, designer trainers, emergency rooms, driving lessons or entertaining her young's unsuitable admirers.

In every other respect, Mrs Blackbird's empty nest syndrome is very similar to that experienced by many mothers (and fathers), who have to make huge adjustments when their little angels grow up and fly off to Thailand on a gap year. For most of us, it is the greatest joy, as well as a worry, raising our families. It is a major step change in life, when they don't seem to need us any more. We, and our own Mr Blackbirds (if we're lucky) suddenly have time for each other again, but we are out of practice and have to remind one another how to be our grown-up, individual selves - Jack and Jill, instead of just Mum and Dad. (You don't have to be Jack and Jill, you will probably have your own names. If you can't remember them, I expect there is an old greeting card somewhere addressed to you both.) Of course, it may only be a brief time, just long enough to solve an irregular sudoku in fact, before the young come flying back with their friends and their laundry, and later their own children. But sometimes we feel too overwhelmed by their departure to celebrate our success as parents and really enjoy the present, as well as look forward to the future.

Then of course, nowadays, there is the opposite syndrome when the chicks get bigger and bigger, some as big as six foot three, with huge feet and equally giant friends, and show no sign of trying out their fluffy, baby wings at all. Maybe the cost of building their own nests is prohibitive, or further education outside the locale is too expensive. Maybe no-one cooks like mum or has a taxi service like dad's either. In any event many households these days are made up of an average of five adults and sometimes, granny or granddad move in too. Even for the most loving families the poor old nest can start splitting at the seams. Then we need to find sensible ways to make sharing our lives comfortable for everyone and sometimes we need to escape into our own worlds and divert ourselves from everyday chores and worries. Whether you have a full nest or an empty nest, make time for yourself - sing on Mrs Blackbird.

HOT TIPS

Empty Nest...

Take a walk in the country and keep on doing it, as often as possible, and listen to Mrs Blackbird singing her little heart out at the sheer joy of being free and alive.

What gets you riled in your neighbourhood? That? Now do something about it, at last! Join an action group, a political party or just your neighbours for a drink.

Become a friend of the local gallery or museum. Volunteer for something that needs your time and experience.

Turn off reality TV and read a book that doesn't start 'Once upon a time ...

Remember when you were eighteen, in the rare moments when you weren't chasing Mr/Miss Blackbird? What happened to the dream of that Ducati/Harley/Honda/BMW or Triumph? And that little boat? And that model aeroplane club? Or better still the flying lessons? Blackbirds are not the only ones with wings!

What attracted you to one another in the first place? Make a list and do it again, or learn something new together; yoga, tantric sex, massage, bungee jumping or para gliding, it doesn't matter what it is, as long as you both enjoy it.

If you liked the look of one another in those motorcycle leathers, or matching woolly jumpers Get the old Hell's Angel chapter together again or brush off your walking boots. Enjoy!

Do you wander lonely as a cloud? Then write a poem, play or story about it. Join your local writers' group. If there isn't one, start your own. If reading is more your style, join a book group. Meet new people who share your interests.

Buy a beret and splash the canvas as an artist. You had those dreams once, dust them off and see if they can't still come true.

Redecorate your home. Keep space for your young to jet in, but don't create shrines to their childhoods. Invite them to help choose the décor for a more adult environment for their frequent and welcome visits. Invite friends to stay or take in lodgers. If your nest seems unbearably empty, look into letting a room to someone else's young; advertise at a local university or college, or consider running a bed and breakfast. Spend the proceeds on yourself.

Buy an MP3 player and download the music you like to listen to and sell all the things you don't need anymore on eBay.

Travel, take a gap year yourselves, two tickets to Rio might cost about the same as keeping a family of four amused during the long summer vacation.

Change your career, or start your own business, you are only responsible to and for yourselves now.

Full nest...

You are never alone with a family, which can be good news and bad news. The rules have changed when your chicks have turned into fledglings and the fledglings are now fully grown and still with you.

Rule number one: Everyone must contribute to the costs. Your cuckoos must contribute at least 20% of their income to the household expenses. It's good for them to learn to pay their way.

Rule number two: Head for the wide-open spaces. They can come and go as they like, but so can you. Neither you nor they are obliged to put dinner on the table every night. No, Mrs B, it isn't your job anymore. Nor are the dishes. Share feasts from time to time but share all the preparation, planning and execution too.

Rule number three: Get organised! Have a family meeting and make sensible rotas to share the chores, guarantee everyone gets time in the bathroom, and that the trash is recycled or collected every week. Share the shopping and the housework. No, home isn't turning into a police state; you people know each other well and can save a lot of heartbreak if you level with one another from the beginning.

Rule number four: If your fledgling's career prospects have hit a brick wall, let him or her know that you will try to help if you are asked, but don't make a bad situation worse by laying it on the line. Hints are better than kicking his or her self-esteem when it's down.

Don't put your dreams on hold! Go away on holiday; write that novel, even if it means building a log cabin in the woods or a shed in the garden to get away from the family.

Respect one another's privacy and space.

Laugh, sing and dance as often as possible.

Birds of a Feather

Here are two lists, which have been muddled up. Can you connect the right collective noun to the right kind of bird?

A siege	of snipe	A fling	of sandpipers
A bellowing	of doves	An exultation	of turtledoves
A wake	of ravens	A wisp	of goldfinches
A clattering	of sparrows	A ubiquity	of eagles
A piteousness	of guillemots	A murmuration	of woodpeckers
A convocation	of swans	A muster	of turkeys
A drum	of bitterns	A flight of	of rooks
A bazaar	of storks	A gargle	of buzzards
A kettle	of thrushes	A mutation	of starlings
A watch	of penguins	A raffle	of bullfinches
A huddle	of hawks	A pitying	of skylarks
An unkindness	of choughs	A descent	of nightingales
A parliament	of swallows		

WORDSEARCH:

Empty Nest/Full Nest

DIVE𝗥SION

```
J Y L Z R D F F H H B L E P
S G W E B A A U T G Y A V R L
P R S X M F Y U J W U Y Z U E
A T O I O S Y Q G N U Y F S A
R C L U U D K C D H O M E I S
E Y P T T E H R A E T U G E U
N J I R I I Y G Z V G E Q L R
T E D W J M N K M W I K R G E
S K C A H I E E U E S R O S E
O E V A R G N I K O O C P E C
N S T A E M O C N I F B F E A
S G H J X P Y H N Z F I E G P
Y S F W G X M R C Q L Y O J S
A K C I Z L H O B B I E S P K
K J I V K T G E L C K P U D B
```

COOKING
DAUGHTERS
FAMILY
HOBBIES
HOME
INCOME
JOY
LAUNDRY
LEISURE
LIFE
PARENTS
PEACE
PLEASURE
PRIVACY
REST
ROUTINE
SHARING
SONS
SPACE
TIME

SUDOKU

Place the numbers 1 to 9 into the grid so that each row, column and marked 3x3 box contains each number once and once only.

9								3
				7				
		3	5	4	6	7		
	4	6	7		1	8	3	
	1						6	
	9	8	3		5	4	2	
		1	8	2	9	5		
				5				
6								8

Hint: Start by looking for numbers that can fit in only one place in a row, column or 3x3 box.

150

SUDOKU

Place the numbers 1 to 9 into the grid so that each row, column and marked 3x3 box contains each number once and once only.

8	3		5		4		1	7
9				8				6
			1		9			
	2						6	
		8				4		
	6						3	
			8		1			
3				9				1
4	5		7		2		9	8

Hint: Start by looking for numbers that can fit in only one place in a row, column or 3x3 box.

KAKURO

Place only the numbers 1 to 9 into the empty white squares so that each across or down run of white squares adds up to the total above or to the left of it. No number can be used more than once in any run, so you cannot use 2 and 2 to add up to '4'. Numbers to the right of the diagonal line give the sum of squares to the right; numbers below the diagonal line give the sum of squares below.

Hint: Start by looking for runs of white squares where only one set of digits will fit, such as 16 (7 and 9) or 17 (8 and 9).

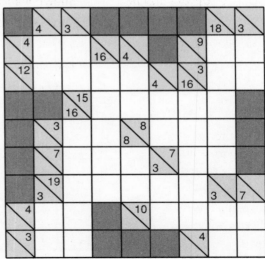

152

Private moments

Create a playlist to escape the full nest or lament the empty one
Here are some ideas to start you off.

Hotel California	The Eagles
Get out	Busta Rhymes
Get out of your lazy bed	Shawn Bianco
Free	Stevie Wonder
Fly like an Eagle	Seal
Leave Home	The Chemical Brothers
She's Leaving Home	The Beatles
Leave Right Now	Will Young
Left Behind	SlipKnot
Living in a Box	Living in a Box

POST HOLIDAY BLUES

Your alarm goes off, you leap out of bed and as you pull up the blinds, your spirits sink. The view from your everyday window can seem deeply depressing after the (delete as applicable) sun, sea, romance, mountains, adventure, wilderness, freedom, culture, relaxation etc of the fabulous holiday from which you have just returned. Strangely, even your lovely, vibrant holiday clothes look sad, as they spill out of your suitcase in a crumpled, grubby heap. The local liqueur you enjoyed each night after dinner, on the golden terrace of that little café under the stars didn't taste so spiffy last night, in the kitchen of your second floor apartment, with the rain beating down outside. The prospect of the commute to the office takes your mood down another degree or two. You hit the snooze button and pull the duvet over your head.

We all need breaks from routine to recharge our batteries and restore our equilibrium, and many of us look forward all year to that annual vacation. We invest it with all sorts of expectations and we can put up with hassle at work and the humdrum at home, as long as we know that our well-deserved break has been planned and booked and we will be leaving all this behind us. Of course, sometimes holidays go wrong and become nightmares, but most of us have a great time, even if we can only afford one (or maybe two at a pinch) holidays a year. When it's over, it seems a very long time to wait until next year. Some unlucky people suffer from 'seasonal affective disorder', in which they become depressed by the short, dark winter days and lack of sunlight. It is only therapy and the promise of that vacation that gets them through the winter.

For the rest of us, it isn't really that bad, but we do often have a bout of the blues in the weeks after a good holiday. So how do you eke out the benefits of your holiday for the rest of the year, beating the gloom, without breaking the bank? The tips below offer some suggestions, but don't forget you can escape from the dullness of the moment by challenging yourself with the diversions that follow. Achieving something, however small, which takes us outside our everyday experience can be like a hit of pure sunshine to our spirits.

HOT TIPS

Take good quality vitamin supplements on your return from holiday, to maintain your immune system against bugs and viruses when you are back in your old routine.

It takes three weeks to form a habit. If you can work hard to keep your stress levels within reasonable bounds for three weeks after your return from holiday, you have a better chance of keeping it up for the rest of the year.

Try to vary your daily routine a little. Take a different route home at least once a week. Go out for a walk at lunchtime. Try to find a park or green space to refresh your spirits.

Do not slip back into the old stress inducing routines. Try to leave work on time. If that isn't possible on a regular basis, keep at least one day a week sacrosanct. Always leave on time that day.

Keep your safely acquired holiday tan, and sun kissed hair topped up, after you return. Revert gradually to your winter plumage.

Don't switch too suddenly from bright, casual holiday clothes to drab everyday outfits as soon as the plane touches down. I'm not suggesting that you wear the same clothes for work as you would on the beach. You can however add a vibrant shirt or blouse to complement a dark suit, or just use a scarf or tie for a touch of cheerful colour, if you feel your colleagues will be rather challenged by the new you. The point is not to give in to the mundane and dull.

Put your holiday snaps on your computer as screensavers, that way you can keep that vacation landscape alive all year.

If you enjoyed the exotic food on holiday, buy a book on that country's cuisine and teach yourself to cook your favourite dishes. Share them with less fortunate friends too, by a having a themed dinner party.

Learn something about the language, and culture so that next time you can take a fuller part in the local life of your favourite places.

Don't revert to couch potato mode as soon as you get home. We do all sorts of things on holiday that we never think about doing at home. If you enjoyed visiting the churches or historic sites, museums and galleries abroad, try exploring those nearer to home. Try to view them as if you were a tourist in your own land.

If you enjoyed outdoor pursuits while you were away, try to find a way to carry them on now you are home. Okay, so sailing on your local dock, skiing indoors and horse riding at a riding school are not the same as the Caribbean, Colorado and the Patagonia respectively, but practice can improve your skills and enhance your enjoyment of your next holiday.

Don't put all your eggs in one basket. Plan a series of shorter breaks throughout the year, especially in the winter months. If you book far enough ahead you can get some good deals on flights and hotels.

Plan some simple treats to keep your spirits up.

Write about your holiday experiences. Start a travel journal or a blog on the Internet.

Never give in to the monotony and drudgery of ordinary life. Make yours spontaneous and fun.

EITHER ...

"Okay, so I wasn't actually the official holiday rep.,but how could I have known that the tee shirt and shorts I grabbed from my bag that bright, sunny morning resembled the uniform that the FabTours girls wore. Yes, I could have just told him he was mistaken when he tapped me on the shoulder, and asked me if he was too late for the excursion to the traditional market and craft workshop. It was just that he looked so anxious and unhappy, and I really didn't have anything planned that day, beyond a long, cool drink by the pool and escape into *Love and Blood* by Evadne Peabody. Alright, alright I lied! In a split second, I had told him that he had missed the rest of the crowd, but we could catch them up. He was so grateful that I'd waited behind for him and full of praise for FabTours. Yeah, I suppose he did look a bit overdressed in his shirt and tie and sports coat with the leather elbow patches. But as he blinked worriedly through those bottle bottom lenses, I thought that his feelings might be hurt if I suggested that he went upstairs to change into something more suitable for the tropical heat. His solar topee was sensible though wasn't it? Anyway, I grabbed my tote and his hand and hopped on to the bus into town. He offered me some of his sandwiches, but I hate the smell of hard-boiled eggs and the crumbs, which clung to his ginger beard made me feel slightly nauseous. I told you, he stopped the bus for a minute to snap the camel train. There's no need to be rude officer, why would I be suspicious? I will come to the station, but what more can I tell you?"...

OR ...

I couldn't wait to pay off the cab and get inside to put my feet up. I knew that I would have to wade through the pile of junk mail and bills that would jam under the front door as soon as I pushed my key into the lock. Rover, my Persian cat (named to frighten burglars) would still be at my mother's house, getting fatter by the second, so no welcoming mews, for me, but I was looking forward to a decent a cup of tea and a long, hot bath. I lugged my suitcase up the front steps, (Yes, chivalry is dead, amongst cab drivers, - in Ruislip anyway) and made my way into the kitchen, carelessly kicking aside the post. Now the kettle whistled and I decided to unpack while I waited for the water to heat up for my bath. If I took out the heavy things down here, I would be able to drag the bag upstairs later. First though, I had to find the little keys that rendered my luggage inviolate to international diamond smugglers and ne'er do wells. I tipped the contents of my purse out on to the carpet and scrabbled amongst the foreign coins and bits of gum, to find the tiny keys. Strangely, they seemed to be missing, just what I needed! Still, I had seen enough police shows to know that a hairpin in the right hands would soon open the locks. I wasn't known as 'Fingers' for nothing! What about luggage tampering? I hear you ask. International diamond smugglers' molls are far too chic to use hairpins, so no danger there. I had no such pretensions however and quickly found one in the muddle on the floor. Forty-five minutes later, the pesky locks yielded to my nimble fingers and the case sprung open. Oh dear! Oh dear, oh dear...

WORDSEARCH:

Post holiday blues

```
S P F R E R A L O N P R N I S
S U I G N I I K S U P O R N H
E S L H S T A O B S Z M I T X
N Q U V S I X M X F X A U J G
I C N R E D I S Y R T N U O C
P I U G F S N A L N Z C W X W
P H S J T I I E U G A E R H R
A U J R K A N O I M N Z C T K
H M O N F H M G P R K I E M A
T P D R I N K I N G F B T R P
S R W P L A N E S A H E N A Y
P S A O A G I Z E O B A W W E
N S O I N N C S T O L C V R Q
Z C I N N S X E O K Z H T A S
L M Q S H S L Q D E Z M H B O
```

BEACH
BOATS
CAMPING
COUNTRYSIDE
DRINKING
EATING
FRIENDSHIP
HAPPINESS
HOTEL
MOUNTAINS
PLANES
ROMANCE
SEA
SKIING
SNOW
SPORTS
SUN
SURFING
TRAINS
WARMTH

KAKURO

Place only the numbers 1 to 9 into the empty white squares so that each across or down run of white squares adds up to the total above or to the left of it. No number can be used more than once in any run, so you cannot use 2 and 2 to add up to '4'. Numbers to the right of the diagonal line give the sum of squares to the right; numbers below the diagonal line give the sum of squares below.

Hint: Start by looking for runs of white squares where only one set of digits will fit, such as 16 (7 and 9) or 17 (8 and 9).

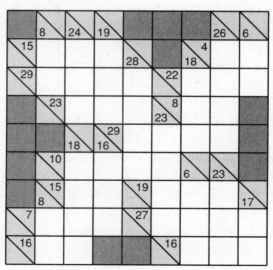

KAKURO

Place only the numbers 1 to 9 into the empty white squares so that each across or down run of white squares adds up to the total above or to the left of it. No number can be used more than once in any run, so you cannot use 2 and 2 to add up to '4'. Numbers to the right of the diagonal line give the sum of squares to the right; numbers below the diagonal line give the sum of squares below.

Hint: Start by looking for runs of white squares where only one set of digits will fit, such as 16 (7 and 9) or 17 (8 and 9).

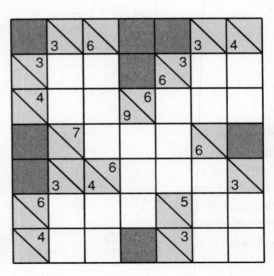

164

SUDOKU

Place the numbers 1 to 9 into the grid so that each row, column and marked 3x3 box contains each number once and once only.

9	2			3			1	8
6		8				5		4
		4				3		
			5		4			
			7	8	2			
			1		3			
		3				9		
2		6				8		5
8	5			7			4	1

Hint: Start by looking for numbers that can fit in only one place in a row, column or 3x3 box.

165

REBUS PUZZLES

The design of the type and its position in the box gives a clue to its
meaning which will be a well-known phrase or saying.

DIET DISASTER

A naughty imp, the enemy of weight watchers everywhere, ambushed you and without so much as by your leave, forced some highly calorific snack into your mouth, thus undoing your entire careful calorie counting for the day. Understandably, you decided that your diet was ruined and although you didn't want to do it, in your disappointment and dismay, you consumed a quart of organic, double chocolate chip, real cream, ice cream with a hand-cut, real potato, deep-fried, French fry chaser. This is not just food; this is fattening food.

This, of course, made you terribly thirsty, and the only drink to hand was a bottle of crisp, cold, white Chardonnay, which you have just shared with a friend. Now you are seriously despondent, and angry with yourself. Whatever next, a baked potato with cheese or a slice of apple pie? Do stop beating yourself up. Even if you have consumed all that, or something very like, your healthy eating regime is not totally wrecked. It is only one day, and maybe your body was craving something sweet after all your self-denial. Actually, nutritionists frown on punishing ourselves for the occasional slip up. It smacks of an unhealthy attitude to food. No food, provided it is not made entirely from cardboard is actually bad. It is the consuming of it in huge quantities and all the time that is not recommended. Some dieticians actually suggest that we give ourselves a treat from time to time, by eating something we really crave, rather than deny ourselves everything we like to eat. We are much less likely to become bored with our diet and thus abandon it altogether. So dry your tears, all is not lost, but if you want to avoid temptation, take a little time to divert yourself from descending the slippery slope. Feed your brain instead of your body when your diet seems to have plateaued out. And pretty soon that imp, who doesn't care much for thinking, will skip off and bother a supermodel instead. Goody!

HOT TIPS

Say this incantation to drive away that naughty imp: A moment on the lips is a lifetime on the hips. He hates it.

Do consult your doctor before you start any radical eating plan or exercise regime.

Take regular exercise, as strangely, not only does it burn up calories, it also makes you feel less hungry. Win win!

Eat a balanced, healthy diet; do not go for a quick fix. Yes you lose weight, but you tend to put it on again and then some, when you stop. Let 'everything in moderation' be your watchword.

Have a selection of seeds and raw vegetables to hand, to pop into your mouth whenever you feel the need.

Drink at least two litres of water a day. Sipping takes the edge off your hunger and cleanses the system of toxins at the same time.

Vary your healthy eating a little. Your body quite quickly adjusts to you eating up to your calorie limit every day, especially if you are eating much the same foods. Shake your metabolism up from time to time. Have a day when you eat only fresh uncooked fruit and vegetables.

Go window-shopping in your lunch hour for some really great clothes, which are the size you hope to be. Promise yourself an outfit as soon as you reach your goal weight. It is good to remind yourself why you doing this.

If you are feeling bored, book a facial and a massage to make you feel really toned. Or get your hair re-styled.

Eat breakfast. It really is good for you and stops that mid-morning snacking urge. Try to eat something with a slow release carbohydrate content. Porridge, or oatmeal is good, served with some fresh berries or a sliced banana.

Try to make your main meal earlier rather than later in the day. Not surprisingly, your body takes longer to metabolise dinner when you are asleep. Also try to avoid the carbs late at night. The processing of carbohydrate makes your body produce more insulin and you wake up feeling hungrier than usual. But don't go to bed hungry.

Avoid sugary snacks and drinks. Water really is a better alternative than artificially sweetened substitutes. They can have an alarming laxative effect when consumed in quantity.

Plan your reward foods into your diet so that you have something to look forward to.

Don't weigh yourself everyday. Your weight will fluctuate according to hormone activity. If you have been very careful, but seem not to have lost an ounce, you will get depressed and are more likely to give up altogether.

Limit your alcohol intake. You may be surprised how many calories there are in wine, beer and spirits.

Do not become obsessed. Food is a pleasure, not a punishment and healthy is good, underweight is not. If you find yourself getting tired and headachy, ask your doctor's advice

Enjoy!

HANJIE

Shade in squares to reveal a hidden picture. The clue numbers to the top and left reveal how many adjacent shaded squares there are in each column and row respectively. If there are multiple numbers for a row or column then there are multiple sequences of adjacent shaded squares with at least one empty square between them, in the order given. For example, "2, 3" would mean that somewhere in that row or column there are 2 adjacent shaded squares, followed by a gap of one or more squares, followed by 3 adjacent shaded squares.

Hint: It's essential to mark in squares you know to be empty with a dot or cross, otherwise you will find it very hard to solve this puzzle! A good tactic is to start by considering the rows and columns with the most shaded squares.

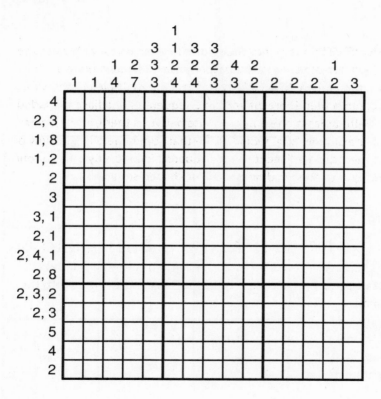

SUDOKU

Place the numbers 1 to 9 into the grid so that each row, column and marked 3x3 box contains each number once and once only.

Hint: Start by looking for numbers that can fit in only one place in a row, column or 3x3 box.

9								6
	8			4			3	
	7		2		8		5	
	1			5			7	
	3		8		7		9	
	4			3			2	
	9		7		1		4	
	6			8			1	
2								7

HITORI

Shade in squares so that no number occurs more than once per row or column. Shaded squares cannot touch in either a horizontal or vertical direction. All unshaded squares must form a single continuous area so that you can move from any unshaded square to any other by travelling only horizontally or vertically between them.

Hint: Circle numbers which must be unshaded in order to keep track of your progress and help see which numbers must be shaded. Start by looking for places where the same number occurs close to itself in a row or column, and considering if anything can be deduced from this.

7	2	6	5	6	3	8	4
2	1	8	5	5	7	4	3
7	5	6	1	6	2	6	8
4	7	5	5	8	7	1	3
7	4	6	3	2	5	6	7
5	8	4	8	3	8	7	2
6	3	6	4	2	1	5	8
5	6	2	7	4	1	3	1

175

HANJIE

Shade in squares to reveal a hidden picture. The clue numbers to the top and left reveal how many adjacent shaded squares there are in each column and row respectively. If there are multiple numbers for a row or column then there are multiple sequences of adjacent shaded squares with at least one empty square between them, in the order given. For example, "2, 3" would mean that somewhere in that row or column there are 2 adjacent shaded squares, followed by a gap of one or more squares, followed by 3 adjacent shaded squares.

Hint: It's essential to mark in squares you know to be empty with a dot or cross, otherwise you will find it very hard to solve this puzzle! A good tactic is to start by considering the rows and columns with the most shaded squares.

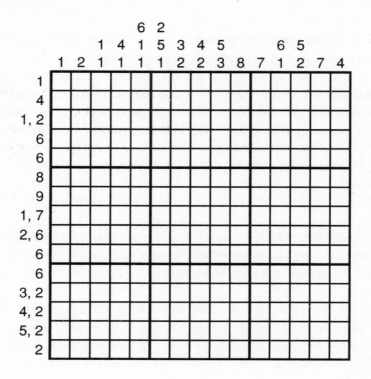

OUTSIDE THE BOX

These are lateral thinking problems so you need to approach them from a different angle. Don't just apply logical, linear thought.

Daylight Robbery: George lives with his parents in London. Last week, while his parents were out, George's next-door neighbor Sophie came round to spend the evening. At one point, she popped out to buy some milk. Just then, two men burst into the apartment and, ignoring George, took the TV set, the stereo and a computer. George had never seen the men before, and they had no legal right to remove the equipment, yet he did nothing to stop them. He didn't even seem surprised by their behaviour. Why not?

Water, Water Everywhere: A woman on a diet goes into a bar and asks for a glass of water. The bartender draws a gun and shoots into the ceiling. The woman thanks him and walks out. Why?

Double Decker: A double-decker London bus has taken a wrong turn and is stuck under a railway bridge. It's just a couple of inches too high to pass under. If the driver can just get free he can get back on to his route and not miss any passengers. An eight-year-old child on the bus saves the day. How?

WORDSEARCH: Diet disaster

```
P Y E Y B B K E E E F S C S S
P A S T R I E S S D N A D L E
Q M X Q T S I R S E R I I E I
J L A Z D C E P R B E M W N R
S T A E R T R E O I W H U D O
T N A E R O W H D Z E T C E L
I I X K T C Y J X S H S M R A
U E N E N D E T A L O C O H C
R J I N R S C C D W A T E R N
F N I A D S U E I H S I F L U
F M T W G R N T V G W W D Z T
X E J E L O Y I E H Q W D H S
S H F K T Y D F R F Y A M S C
R H H S K Z W A F I W M D Y U
M X R V A P Z A G V W B J A S
```

BERRIES
CALORIES
CARBOHYDRATES
CHEESE
CHOCOLATE
EXERCISE
FISH
FIT
FRUIT
ICE-CREAM
NUTS
PASTRIES
PROTEIN
SEEDS
SLENDER
SLIM
TONED
TREATS
WATER
WINE

THE END OF THE AFFAIR

You can't eat or sleep, your concentration is shot to pieces, and yet you feel fantastic, fizzing with excitement and overcome with feelings of intense joy in all you see, and goodwill to all your fellow men. You have fallen in love, and the object of your affections is perfect in every respect. No man or woman has ever been more handsome or beautiful, a more accomplished lover, witty, kind and fun. This thing, as the cliché would have it, is bigger than both of you, irresistible, and overpowering, you can't be separated for a minute, and love is the most exhilarating, glorious feeling in the world.

You still can't sleep, but you can't stop eating, your concentration is lousy and you feel terrible. The sight of lovers entwined in the park fills you with simmering rage and the cheesiest songs reduce you to tears of despair. You are still in love, but this time you are in it on your own. Your god or goddess of love has unaccountably changed his or her mind and gone off in search of real love. You are heartbroken, but you are not alone. If you have managed to reach adulthood without having your heart broken before, or at least severely dented, you are a very rare bird indeed, or you come from another planet, like Mars or Venus. Life and literature; music, film, and art are full of star-crossed couples, misunderstandings, sacrifices, heartbreak and doomed love. Since we are designed to attract one another, it seems extraordinary that evolution hasn't taught us how to get better at charting the treacherous waters of love without getting wrecked on the rocks of unrealistic expectations.

I am not going to tell you that falling in love isn't wonderful and offer you hot tips on how to avoid it. For every broken heart, there are daily reminders of those people who, in happy old age, are still living happily ever after. Some may even get it right first time, but most will have taken a while to find that perfect combination of passion and fidelity, unconditional love and compatibility that we all seek. Just now you need to divert yourself from all this pain and give time, that other great cliché, free rein to do that thing it does so well – heal! Falling in love is the best feeling in the world, and believe me, no matter how bad you are feeling at this minute, however angry, hurt and rejected, you will fall in love again, and when you do you will not be able to eat (hurrah!) or sleep, your concentration will be shot to pieces, and yet...

HOT TIPS

Boil no bunnies.

Please try the breathing and relaxation exercise on page 12-17, when you feel yourself losing control of your emotions.

By all means, read all those love letters or texts whilst looking at his or her picture and listening to 'All by myself' and every other sad song you can find. Rent some really schmaltzy movies and eat ice cream, just like they do on the screen. If you cry, so much the better, but set a time limit on wallowing in your misery. After two days, consider drying your eyes and giving yourself a bit of a talking to.

Take that by now familiar large sheet of paper and make a list of the things you really loved about the ex love of your life. Be honest, even if it hurts. Now write down all the things he or she did, however small, that made you crazy. I would wager a small sum that if you are truthful about this, the lists would be roughly equal. Yes, you loved him or her, but see, he or she wasn't perfect. There was a human being there not a god or goddess.

Now, take another sheet of paper and write a list of your ten best qualities. No one is going to see this list, you can be honest here. Write another list of the ten things you would like to change. Be sensible, new feet or bigger ears are not an option. Make a conscious effort to write only those things which are possible and which you feel would genuinely make you happier. Aim to change a maximum of five per cent of them in the next twelve months. The aim is to love yourself, before you expect any one else to love you.

Take care of yourself, book into a spa for the weekend and treat yourself to some really luxurious treatments. At the very least book a body massage. If spas are not your cup of tea, book a weekend away by the sea. Make sure that the place where you are staying has a first class chef, a comfortable bed and a great view. Take that really good book that you have been meaning to read with you.

Don't leap into another relationship on the rebound. Don't use someone else like a band-aid to heal your wounded pride. Give yourself at least three months before you start dating seriously again.

Exorcise your space. Throw away all those things you had around for your lover, but never really liked. This includes uncomfortable lingerie and designer shorts. Redecorate, or at the very least re-arrange the furniture,

Get some exercise in the fresh air. The combination really does release endorphins, which will make you feel happier.

Try to get plenty of rest. I know it can be hard to sleep when your heart is aching, but every time you wake in the morning, you will feel a tiny bit better.

Think positive and practise the visualisation exercises at the front of this book. See yourself as peaceful and happy. Write down some affirmations on post it notes. They should reinforce your most positive feelings about yourself.

Give the ice cream a miss after the first two days, the sugar high will wear off and give you a corresponding low.

Avoid alcohol, it will only make you feel maudlin and encourage tears.

Contact those friends you may have been neglecting and make it up to them.

Buy yourself some flowers and take each day as it comes, one at a time.

Try to treat this affair as a learning experience. Could you have misjudged things here?

Do not run straight into the arms of his or her best friend, however sympathetic they might seem.

Use your brain and your body to soothe and heal your wounded spirit.

WORDSEARCH:

The end of the affair

```
T O X E R L H D R P D D E J M
V O V A E I I J I L E F T E A
J O J T V S A H E N S D A Z F
L O T B T O S F W K S E N E F
V E D A E D N O F I O N O B P
R O N E N A N A N A R T I E L
X C V E T K U F S Y C I S L U
E E I T N I M T F A U C S R C
K R C U V C U Y I V C I A A M
F T E R C E S Q S F T N P T G
E M O S D N A H E T U G B S E
P O P U L A R U Y R E L V U T
S E D U C T I V E E N R D Z A
N O I T A N I G A M I U Y Y E
C G U H W V V K J Y Q N L V A
```

AFFAIR
BEAUTIFUL
CASANOVA
DISTANCE
ENTICING
FRIENDSHIP
HANDSOME
IMAGINATION
JEZEBEL
LOVE/LETTER
MYSTERY
PASSIONATE
POPULAR
SECRET
SEDUCTIVE
STAR/CROSSED
UNKNOWN
UNREQUITED

SUDOKU

Place the numbers 1 to 9 into the grid so that each row, column and marked 3x3 box contains each number once and once only.

		1	7		6	8		
	6	9				7	1	
5								3
			1		9			
6			3		5			2
			2		8			
1								8
	9	5				2	3	
		3	8		7	5		

Hint: Start by looking for numbers that can fit in only one place in a row, column or 3x3 box.

HANJIE

Shade in squares to reveal a hidden picture. The clue numbers to the top and left reveal how many adjacent shaded squares there are in each column and row respectively. If there are multiple numbers for a row or column then there are multiple sequences of adjacent shaded squares with at least one empty square between them, in the order given. For example, "2, 3" would mean that somewhere in that row or column there are 2 adjacent shaded squares, followed by a gap of one or more squares, followed by 3 adjacent shaded squares.

Hint: It's essential to mark in squares you know to be empty with a dot or cross, otherwise you will find it very hard to solve this puzzle! A good tactic is to start by considering the rows and columns with the most shaded squares.

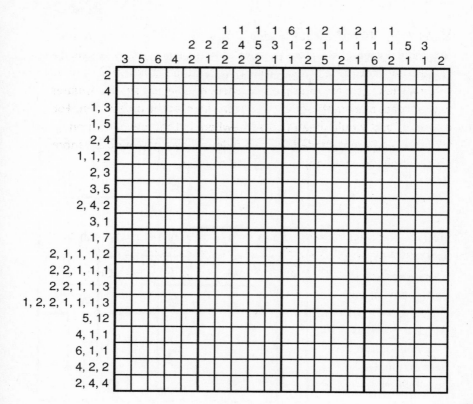

IRREGULAR SUDOKU

Place the numbers 1 to 9 into the grid so that each row, column and bold shape contains each number once and once only.

Hint: You can sometimes use the widest part of each shape, and the way in which it overlaps with a row or column, to help eliminate possibilities.

		5				7		
			9					
	8	7		2		5	6	
7		4				2		1
	3	2		5		1	4	
				3				
		6				9		

SLITHERLINK

Draw a single loop by joining the dots with straight horizontal or vertical lines. Each number specifies how many adjacent dots must be joined in the 'square' around that number. Areas without numbers can have any number of dots joined. The loop cannot touch or cross over itself.

Hint: Start by considering the corners and the o and 3 'squares'. Mark the areas between dots that you deduce must not be joined with a small 'x'.

```
.   .   .   .   .   .   .   .   .   .   .
    2       1       1
.   .   .   .   .   .   .   .   .   .   .
    0           1       3   2       1   1
.   .   .   .   .   .   .   .   .   .   .
  3   1       1       1       2       1
.   .   .   .   .   .   .   .   .   .   .
    0       0               0       2
.   .   .   .   .   .   .   .   .   .   .
  1       0               3       1
.   .   .   .   .   .   .   .   .   .   .
  3       2       3       2       0   3
.   .   .   .   .   .   .   .   .   .   .
  2   1       1   2       2       2
.   .   .   .   .   .   .   .   .   .   .
                    1       2       2
.   .   .   .   .   .   .   .   .   .   .
```

DAY ONE VERY NAUGHTY
CHOCOLATE SAUCE

While you are eating that ice-cream, why not add some extremely naughty chocolate sauce?

Making it takes only minutes, and chocolate triggers the same hormone that gets us feeling all romantic when we fall in love, so you won't feel so bereft. Quantities are very rough, since you can adjust to taste. Do this only once!

2 oz butter
1 tablespoon cocoa powder
1 tablespoon golden syrup or light corn syrup
2 teaspoons water.

In a small heavy based pan, melt the butter over a low heat.
Stir in the cocoa powder.
Stir in the golden syrup or light corn syrup
Add the water.
Keep stirring until all the ingredients have combined.
Pour over the ice cream of your choice and eat.

GINGERBREAD REVENGE

This is a perfectly harmless, quite silly, but quite satisfying mild voodoo revenge. Make some gingerbread men or women, according to the gender of your heartbreaker. As you take bites out of them and encourage your friends to do the same, imagine that he or she is experiencing little nips like insect bites on the appropriate parts of his or her anatomy and that all the calories that you are consuming are being transferred immediately to his or her bottom.

2 oz butter
2 oz sugar
1 tablespoon golden syrup or light corn syrup
6 oz/1 cup self-raising flour
1 teaspoon bicarbonate of soda
1 rounded teaspoon ground ginger

Pre-heat oven to gas mark 5, 375° F (190° C)
Lightly grease a baking tray

Melt the butter, sugar and syrup in a pan stirring occasionally. Remove from the heat. Sift the flour, bicarbonate of soda and ground ginger into a large bowl. Mix the syrup mixture into the flour mixture, until you have a fairly stiff dough. Turn out on to a lightly floured surface and roll out to a thickness of about 1/4 inch.

Dip the edges of your gingerbread man cutter in flour and cut out the shape. You may find you have to roll out the dough a couple of times to get four or five biscuits. Use a palette knife to lift them on to the baking tray. Use raisins to make the eyes and buttons of your gingerbread men and then bake in the oven for eight to ten minutes until a lovely golden brown. Let them cool until hard on the baking tray and then transfer onto a cooling rack.

If you have some tubes of icing, you can add attractive tattoos and small blemishes. Decide whether to eat the head first, so he or she can't shout at you or the feet so that he or she can't run away. Or you could nibble the knees, so that there can be no last minute begging for you to take him or her back.

BROKEN-HEARTED PLAYLIST

Create a playlist of songs to make you laugh or cry
Here are some ideas to get you started.

Heartbreak Hotel	Elvis Presley
What becomes of the broken-hearted?	Jimmy Ruffin
The tears of a clown	Smokey Robinson/Miracles
You don't have to say you love me	Dusty Springfield
It's my party and I'll cry if I want to	Lesley Gore
If I fell	The Beatles
In my life	The Beatles
Without you	Nilsson
Cathy's Clown	The Everley Brothers
If you leave me now	Bread

SOLUTIONS

The solutions are given in their chapters
in the order they appear in the book.

DEAD END JOB

SUDOKU

6	3	4	5	7	8	1	9	2
2	1	8	4	9	3	7	6	5
7	5	9	6	1	2	3	8	4
1	7	6	3	4	9	2	5	8
3	9	2	8	5	1	6	4	7
8	4	5	2	6	7	9	1	3
4	6	1	7	3	5	8	2	9
9	8	3	1	2	4	5	7	6
5	2	7	9	8	6	4	3	1

WORDSEARCH: Dream jobs

```
+ L + + R + D N + D + + N + L
R + A O + E + A R + R U + R E
+ A T W N + + I + E R + E J D
R C T T Y + V C T S H K + U O
A E I S + E + I E + A C + D M
+ S M + R + R T + M A + A G +
T + + A + W + I M + S + + E +
K C O R T P I L O T T R D + T
+ + + + N I O + + R E O + +
R E C I F F O P + + O C C + +
+ E X E C U T I V E N N T + +
A R T I S T + R L + A A O + +
+ E C I L O P + A + U D R + +
+ + + + + + + + I T + + + +
+ + + + + + + + + N + + + +
```

(Over,down,direction)
ACTOR(1,5,NE)
ARTIST(1,12,E)
ASTRONAUT(11,6,S)
DANCER(12,13,N)
DENTIST(7,1,SW)
DOCTOR(13,8,S)
DRIVER(10,1,SW)
EXECUTIVE(2,11,E)
FILMMAKER(6,10,NE)
JUDGE(14,3,S)
LAWYER(2,1,SE)
LION-TAMER(9,12,NW)
MODEL(15,5,N)
NURSE(13,1,SW)
OFFICER(7,10,W)
PILOT(6,8,E)
POLICE(7,13,W)
POLITICIAN(8,10,N)
ROCK(4,8,W)
STAR(4,5,NW)
TEACHER(15,8,NW)
TRAIN(7,11,SE)
WRITER(6,7,NE)

ACRONYMS

AAPNAC	Always A Pleasure Never A Chore
AONAO	An Opportunity Not An Obstacle
CRAFT	Can't Remember A Flipping Thing
DIN	Do It Now
DRIB	Don't Read If Busy
EBOM	Engage Brain, Open Mouth
GROW	Goals, Reality, Options, Will
KASH	Knowledge, Attitude, Skills, Habits
MBWA	Management By Wandering About
NAP	Not A Problem
SEP	Someone Else's Problem
SUMO	Shut Up, Move On
SWOT	Strengths, Weaknesses, Opportunities, Threats
USP	Unique Selling Point
WYGIWYE	What You Get Is What You Expect

HANJIE

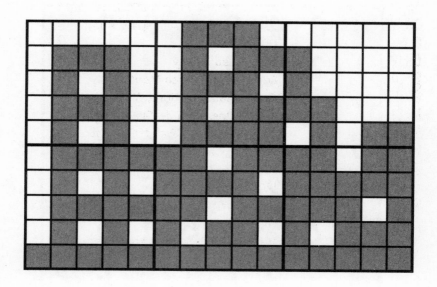

HITORI

8	8	4	6	6	3	5	1
1	2	7	5	7	4	7	6
7	8	6	1	4	2	8	1
5	6	3	2	4	8	3	7
4	1	2	7	8	6	7	3
5	7	5	3	5	1	6	4
6	5	8	7	1	6	2	3
3	4	3	1	3	2	3	5

CANCELLED FLIGHT

WORDSEARCH: Cancelled Flight

```
L E P L U B N A T S I D S + +
+ A U A + + O + + + + A + + +
+ + E G R G A I C U L D + + +
+ + + R A I + + E L + I + + +
+ + + C T R S B A M + N S + +
+ + I L + N P D A + O I + A +
+ H + O + + O D A N L R + + N
C T + N + + R M + A G T + + I
K O + D + I S + B + + K + + A
R K + O D T S Y D N E Y O + B
O Y + N E T O R O N T O C K M
Y O + R N O B S I L + A + + U
+ + D N E W + + + + I + + + M
+ A + + + + + + + R + + + + +
M + + + + + + + O + + + + + +
```

(Over,Down,Direction)
AMSTERDAM(9,7,SW)
BALI(9,9,NE)
BANGKOK(8,5,SE)
CAIRO(13,11,SW)
CHICAGO(1,8,NE)
DALLAS(8,6,NE)
ISTANBUL(11,1,W)
LISBON(10,12,W)
LONDON(4,6,S)
MADRID(10,5,SW)
MONTREAL(8,8,NW)
MUMBAI(15,13,N)
NEW(4,13,E)
PARIS(3,1,SE)
PRAGUE(7,6,NW)
ROME(12,7,NW)
SYDNEY(7,10,E)
TOKYO(2,8,S)
TORONTO(6,11,E)
TRINIDAD(12,8,N)
YORK(1,12,N)

HITORI

6	8	6	2	4	5	7	7
7	7	6	7	2	8	3	1
3	4	4	8	5	4	2	7
4	5	3	6	1	1	3	4
1	8	5	4	6	4	8	3
7	2	4	1	1	3	1	6
2	2	7	5	8	5	4	5
7	6	8	3	1	5	1	2

IRREGULAR SUDOKU

3	9	6	7	2	1	4	5	8
1	5	9	3	8	2	7	6	4
8	7	2	6	4	5	1	9	3
6	8	5	9	3	4	2	7	1
2	4	3	8	5	9	6	1	7
4	3	7	1	6	8	5	2	9
9	6	1	2	7	3	8	4	5
7	1	4	5	9	6	3	8	2
5	2	8	4	1	7	9	3	6

KAKURO

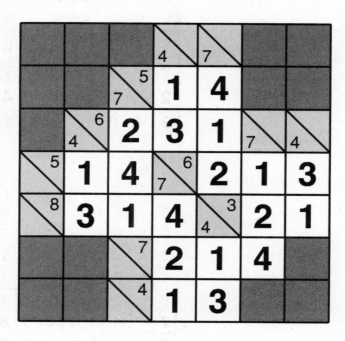

REBUS PUZZLES

RI BS   = Broken ribs

WON
  ONE   = Odd one out
WON

E E
 Y   = Crossed Eyes
E E

FLYER   = High Flyer

RA   = Race against time
AM
CP
EM

LIFE11TIME   = once (ones) in a lifetime

MOVING ON

WORDSEARCH: Moving on

```
G + + + + S + D + + R L F O +
N + + + + + U + E O + E R P +
I L A W E N E R M C + V I P +
S F A M I L Y A P E O A E O +
N + + + H + N W X R + R N R +
A + + O E C + C E Y I T D T +
E + M + E G I + R N + S S U +
L E E R U T N E V D A R E N L
C E + + E + V E + + E + + I O
+ + G M + O + + L E + + + T V
+ + E N C + + + R L + + + Y E
+ N + S A + + A + + A + + + +
T + I + + H C L A U G H T E R
+ D + + + + C + + + + + C + +
+ + + + + + + + N U F + + + +
```

(Over, Down, Direction)
ADVENTURE (11,8,W)
CAREER (7,13,NE)
CHALLENGE (13,14,NW)
CHANGE (7,14,NW)
CLEANSING (1,9,N)
DECOR (8,1,SE)
DISCOVERY (2,14,NE)
EXCITEMENT (10,4,SW)
FAMILY (2,4,E)
FRIENDS (13,1,S)
FUN (11,15,W)
HOME (5,5,SW)
LAUGHTER (8,13,E)
LOVE (15,8,S)
NEW (10,7,NW)
OPPORTUNITY (14,1,S)
RENEWAL (8,3,W)
ROMANCE (11,1,SW)
SURPRISE (6,1,SE)
TRAVEL (12,6,N)

SLITHERLINK

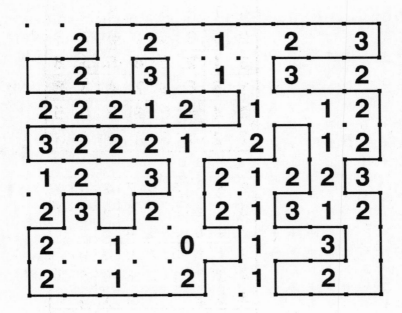

HITORI

8	3	5	3	6	7	2	2
8	8	7	1	3	1	5	2
4	7	2	5	4	6	3	4
2	5	8	5	1	5	7	3
3	1	2	6	4	5	2	8
1	5	6	3	7	4	8	3
3	4	6	8	6	2	6	5
7	2	1	3	8	4	4	3

SUDOKU

9	6	1	3	5	7	2	8	4
3	5	4	2	8	1	6	7	9
7	2	8	9	6	4	5	3	1
2	1	6	5	4	8	3	9	7
4	3	7	1	9	6	8	5	2
5	8	9	7	3	2	1	4	6
1	9	5	4	2	3	7	6	8
8	4	2	6	7	5	9	1	3
6	7	3	8	1	9	4	2	5

KAKURO

AGENT-SPEAK CRYPTOGRAMS

```
A B C D E F G H I J K L M N O P Q R S T U V W X Y Z
N O P Q R S T U V W X Y Z A B C D E F G H I J K L M
```
Alphabet moved down half way

```
        B I J O U X
        O V W B H K = SMALL
```

```
A B C D E F G H I J K L M N O P Q R S T U V W X Y Z
O N P Q U R S T A V W X Y Z E B C D F G I H J K L M
```
Vowels moved down 2 and consonants started at N

```
        U N S P O I L E D
        I B F B E A X U Q = UNMODERNISED
```

```
A B C D E F G H I J K L M N O P Q R S T U V W X Y Z
N A O B P C Q D R E S F T G U H V I W J X K Y L Z M
```
Alphabet moved replacing every other letter begin with skip one A,
skip another B etc and then around to the beginning of the alphabet

```
        C H A R M I N G
        O D N I T R G Q = STRANGE
```

A B C D E F G H I J K L M N O P Q R S T U V W X Y Z
B A Z Y X W V U T S R Q P O N M L K J I H G F E S C
The alphabet is reversed starting at C

            C O M P A C T
            Z N P M B Z I = REALLY TINY

A B C D E F G H I J K L M N O P Q R S T U V W X Y Z
U Z Y X O W V T I S R Q P N E M L K J H A G F D C B
Vowels are reversed A = U as are the consonants B=Z

            E X Q U I S I T E
            O D L A I J I H O = FUSSY

A B C D E F G H I J K L M N O P Q R S T U V W X Y Z
N A O B P C Q D R E S F T G U H V I W J X K Y L Z M
Alphabet moved replacing every other letter begin with skip one A, skip
another B etc and then around to the beginning of the alphabet

            M I N I M A L I S T
            T R G R T N F R W J = EMPTY

HOME ALONE

WORDSEARCH: Home alone

```
R  S  +  W  +  +  +  +  +  +  T  G  +  B  T
E  +  I  +  A  +  +  A  +  E  +  O  +  O  +
L  +  +  G  +  L  M  A  L  +  +  U  U  O  +
A  +  +  G  H  E  K  E  P  +  +  R  +  K  +
X  +  +  +  N  T  V  I  +  S  I  M  +  S  S
A  +  S  I  +  I  S  +  N  S  +  E  +  P  E
T  +  C  L  S  +  L  E  M  G  +  T  O  +  R
I  +  +  I  E  +  E  C  E  +  +  R  Y  E  U
O  D  O  O  F  E  +  S  Y  I  T  +  R  +  C
N  N  +  +  +  P  +  I  C  N  U  U  +  I
G  N  I  N  E  D  R  A  G  C  C  G  X  +  N
S  W  I  M  M  I  N  G  +  I  R  +  U  +  A
E  R  T  A  E  H  T  +  D  +  +  E  L  +  M
+  +  P  E  A  C  E  E  +  +  +  +  X  +  +
+  +  +  +  +  +  P  +  +  +  +  +  E  +
```

(Over,Down,Direction)
BOOKS(14,1,S)
CINEMA(3,7,NE)
CYCLING(10,10,NW)
EXERCISE(14,15,NW)
FOOD(5,9,W)
GARDENING(9,11,W)
GOURMET(12,1,S)
LUXURY(13,13,N)
MANICURE(15,13,N)
PEACE(3,14,E)
PEDICURE(7,15,NE)
RELAXATION(1,1,S)
SIGHTSEEING(2,1,SE)
SLEEP(3,6,SE)
SPA(10,5,NW)
SPORT(15,5,SW)
SWIMMING(1,12,E)
TELEVISION(11,1,SW)
THEATRE(7,13,W)
TOURISM(15,1,SW)
WALKING(4,1,SE)

HANJIE

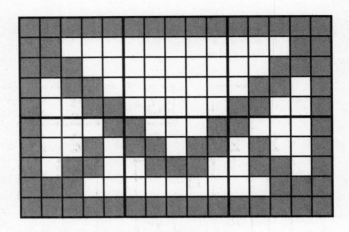

HITORI

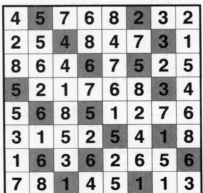

4	5	7	6	8	2	3	2
2	5	4	8	4	7	3	1
8	6	4	6	7	5	2	5
5	2	1	7	6	8	3	4
5	6	8	5	1	2	7	6
3	1	5	2	5	4	1	8
1	6	3	6	2	6	5	6
7	8	1	4	5	1	1	3

SLITHERLINK

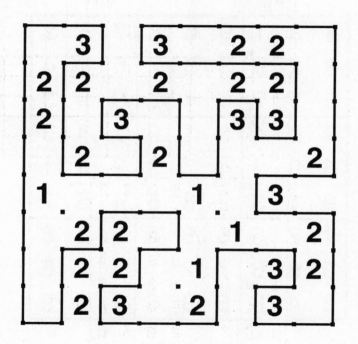

SUDOKU

4	3	1	9	6	8	7	5	2
8	2	9	3	5	7	6	1	4
6	5	7	1	4	2	8	9	3
7	8	4	6	1	9	2	3	5
5	6	2	4	7	3	9	8	1
9	1	3	2	8	5	4	6	7
1	7	5	8	9	4	3	2	6
3	9	6	7	2	1	5	4	8
2	4	8	5	3	6	1	7	9

REBUS PUZZLES

TLUASREMOS	=	Backward somersault
•2•	=	Point to point
mod con mod con mod con mod con mod con mod con mod con mod con	=	all mod cons
live live live live day day	=	Live for today (Live 4 2 Day)

BAD DATE SYNDROME

Would like to meet

GSOH	Good Sense Of Humour
OIOH	One Income Own Home
GFAW	Good Food And Wine
FVF	Fun View Friendship
GM/GW	Gay Man /Gay Woman
OHAT	Own Hair And Teeth
LAF	Loving And Faithful
BAV	Born Again Virgin
NB	No Baggage
OG/OB	Outdoor Girl/ Outdoor Boy
TDAH	Tall Dark And Handsome
KIR	Keep It Real

WORDSEARCH: Bad date syndrome

```
+ + P + R E + + + D + L M F E
+ N + E S U R + R + A + O L N
+ + U N R E O I + N + + V O I
+ + E F L F V M O + + + I W T
+ S + A + E E S U + + + E E N
S + X + + R C + H + + + R E L
+ E + + + E + + T + + + + S L
D + T + P S S I M + + + + + A
R + + A P I H S D N E I R F V
E + + + L + + + + + + + + + +
N + + + + O G N I D D E W + +
N + + + + + C R O M A N T I C
I R I G H T + O R M + T + + +
D + + + + + + + H + + + E + +
+ + + + + + + + + C + + + S +
```

(Over,Down,Direction)
CHOCOLATES(10,15,NW)
DATES(10,11,SE)
DINNER(1,14,N)
DRIVE(10,1,SW)
FLOWERS(14,1,S)
FRIENDSHIP(14,9,W)
FUN(4,4,NW)
HUMOUR(10,6,NW)
MISS(9,8,W)
MOVIE(13,1,S)
MR (10,13,W)
OF (7,3,SW)
PERFECT(3,1,SE)
PERSONAL(5,8,NE)
RELAXED(7,2,SW)
RIGHT(2,13,E)
ROMANTIC(8,12,E)
SENSE(2,5,NE)
VALENTINE(15,9,N)
WEDDING(13,11,W)

HITORI

1	2	4	7	8	7	3	7
8	7	6	5	6	1	2	8
6	4	3	7	2	4	1	8
8	1	5	3	5	2	2	6
3	4	8	4	7	7	6	1
7	8	1	6	3	5	4	8
4	7	7	7	1	3	4	2
7	3	1	2	6	8	7	4

KAKURO

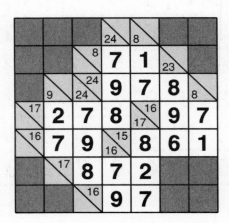

IRREGULAR SUDOKU

8	3	5	7	2	6	1	9	4
7	9	1	8	3	5	2	4	6
4	2	6	5	8	7	9	3	1
2	6	3	4	1	9	5	8	7
9	7	8	1	4	3	6	2	5
6	4	7	2	9	1	8	5	3
3	8	9	6	5	4	7	1	2
1	5	2	3	6	8	4	7	9
5	1	4	9	7	2	3	6	8

IRREGULAR SUDOKU

4	2	8	7	1	9	6	3	5
9	6	3	1	5	8	7	4	2
5	3	4	2	7	6	9	8	1
1	7	5	4	3	2	8	9	6
2	9	1	3	6	4	5	7	8
6	8	7	9	2	1	3	5	4
8	4	2	5	9	3	1	6	7
3	5	6	8	4	7	2	1	9
7	1	9	6	8	5	4	2	3

WHAT IS WRONG WITH THIS ALPHABET?

The O is a zero (0)

SOCIAL DILEMMAS

Switched on
Switch one light on for a minute; turn it off and turn another on. Go into the room and feel the off-bulbs. The warm one is connected to the first switch, the on-bulb is connected to the second.

The tyres they are a-changing
Take one nut off each of the other three wheels and put them on the spare.

REBUS PUZZLES

DNUORG WORK	=	Background work
OCEDROPAN	=	A drop in the ocean

RAIN
PRAY RAIN
     RAIN
     RAIN
	=	Pray fo(u)r rain

S U N	=	Sundown
N U S	=	Sun up

ADOLESCENCE: IT'S PMS

WORSEARCH: Adolescence

```
T + + N O I H S A F G + + + +
M N + + + + E C H A N G E + +
U + E + + N + + M + + + + D +
S + + M O S N E E T + + A + Y
I + + M E + S + + + + N + + T
C + R S + T + L + + C + Y + I
+ O P + C + I + O I + G + + S
H + R S I H + C N O R S + + N
+ + I + T N O G X E C E W + E
+ + V + + N T O N E + H E + T
+ + A + + + E E L + + T N + N
+ + C + + + + R R + + O + + I
+ + Y + + + + + A N + L + + +
Y T I R A L U P O P E C + + +
S H O P P I N G + + + T + + +
```

(Over,Down,Direction)
CHANGE(8,2,E)
CLOTHES(12,14,N)
COOL(11,9,NW)
DANCING(14,3,SW)
ENERGY(8,11,NE)
EXCITEMENT(10,10,NW)
FASHION(10,1,W)
GAMES(11,1,SW)
HORMONES(1,8,NE)
INTENSITY(15,12,N)
INTERNET(5,8,SE)
MUSIC(1,2,S)
NEW(13,11,N)
PARENTS(10,14,NW)
POPULARITY(10,14,W)
PRIVACY(3,7,S)
SCHOOL(4,6,SE)
SHOPPING(1,15,E)
TEENS(10,4,W)

225

URGR8

BETBstUCnBE

Be The Best You Can Be

EvrEDAInEvrEWAURGttnBTa&BTa
Every Day In Every Way You Are Getting Better and Better

ULkGR8

You Look Great

HIMmImSAf

Hi Mum I am Safe

ShnOnSpaS*

Shine on Superstar

UcnDoIt

You Can Do It

ILuvU

I Love You

DntWrEBHaPE

Don't Worry Be Happy

URBUtifl

You Are Beautiful

NvaSANva

Never Say Never

SUDOKU

1	2	4	3	5	8	6	7	9
9	5	8	4	6	7	2	3	1
7	6	3	9	2	1	4	8	5
3	8	5	2	9	4	1	6	7
6	9	1	7	8	5	3	2	4
2	4	7	1	3	6	5	9	8
4	1	6	8	7	2	9	5	3
8	3	2	5	4	9	7	1	6
5	7	9	6	1	3	8	4	2

SLITHERLINK

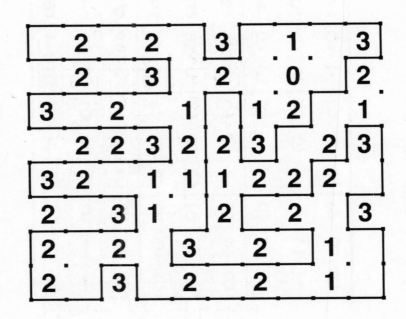

KAKURO

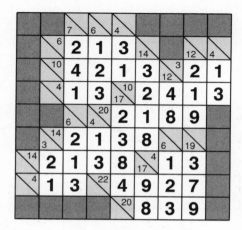

HANJIE

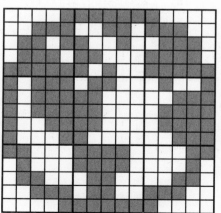

REBUS PUZZLES

EVER	=	for (4) ever
EVER		
EVER		
EVER		

NA	=	Run up And down
UN		
RD		

GONE	=	For(4)gone conclusions
GONE END		
GONE		
GONE		

IDEA	=	Big idea

MYSTERY IN THE MIDDLE

Dotherboys Orphanage
Code: Capital letters
Message:
Where are Nutkin's widow and child?

The Healthy Badger Society
Code: Missing letters
Message:
Nutkin was left to die

The Blue Ribbon Charity – to find a cure for Prostate Cancer
Code: –Vowels do not make sense as the vowels are switched with 3rd
one along
Hu as net fegettun
A E I O U
O U A E I
Message:
He is not forgotten

Single Mums Stranded in Bognor Appeal
Code: Some consonants do not make sense as the alphabet is reversed
Thus ponec fiqq noh jage cou'
bcdfghjklmnpqrstvwxyz
zyxw vtsrqpnmlkjhgfdcb
Message:
Money will not save you

Society for Environmentally Friendly Interments
Code: Letters in capitals
Message:
IT IS YOUR TURN TO DIE

The full story

With Guy and Stacy's help, the police were able to unmask the
murderer of Sir Orphington Sprogg as none other than George Nutkin.
Sir Orphington was indeed a fantastically wealthy man, who had made
his money from a gold strike in Canada in 1966. He had re-opened an
old mine on the insistence of his business partner, Jim Nutkin. While
they were secretly inspecting the mine after the first reports that gold
had been found, the two men became separated in the maze of
tunnels.

Sir Orphington heard a terrific crash as the roof collapsed ahead of him trapping Jim in the tunnel. Sir Orphington escaped, and since no one knew that they were there, he left Jim to die in the mine. He claimed later that Jim had disappeared with the first nuggets of gold, and enquiries had never revealed his whereabouts.

Sir Orphington did not know that Jim had a wife and infant son. The wife believed that her husband had deserted her and brought the child up in poverty.

In 2006, George discovered that a skeleton had been found at the mine, which was thought to be a mine worker. George believed it to be his father and driven mad with fury, he began his campaign to torment Sir Orphington and ultimately kill him, as his father had been killed.

George was caught after Guy and Stacy traced the source of the trail of emails through the Internet cafes of small, south coast sea side towns in England. He confessed to his crime and Sir Orphington's private papers subsequently revealed the truth about Jim Nutkin's death. He had been racked with guilt because, motivated by greed he had left Jim to die. He had spent his life trying to give the tainted money away. George is now serving life in Broadmoor.

MIDDLESCENCE

KAKURO

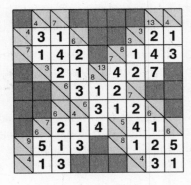

HANJIE

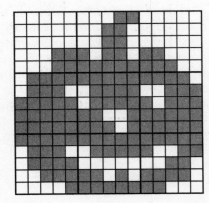

SLITHERLINK

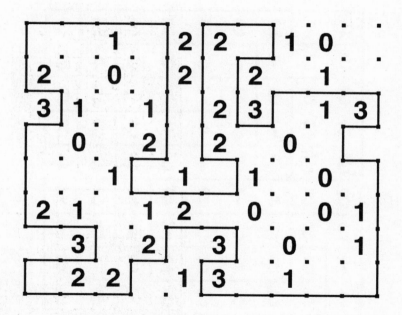

IRREGULAR SUDOKU

4	1	2	9	8	5	6	7	3
5	3	1	7	6	8	9	4	2
3	8	9	2	7	4	1	5	6
6	2	7	5	4	1	3	9	8
9	7	5	6	1	3	8	2	4
8	5	4	1	9	6	2	3	7
2	9	6	3	5	7	4	8	1
7	6	8	4	3	2	5	1	9
1	4	3	8	2	9	7	6	5

WORDSEARCH: Middlescence

```
R P + + + E + + + + + + + +
E E + + + X + + H A I R C U T
S N L + + P + + + + + O + B +
I S + A + E + S + + S + + O +
C I + + T R N N + M + + + T +
R O + + + I + S E N O M R O H
E N + + M E O T P G + F + X +
X + H A + N I N R O A + + + +
E S T E P C + E S S T L + + +
+ I L R S E E + H H T I L + +
V + A + A R + I + + I N O O +
+ + E + A V O + + + C P I N C
+ + H C + N E + + A + + S O S
E R U S I E L L S + + + + + J
F A M I L Y + H + + + + + + +
```

(Over, Down, Direction)

BOTOX(14,3,S)
CAREER(4,13,NE)
CASH(11,12,SW)
COLLAGEN(15,12,NW)
COSMETICS(13,2,SW)
EXERCISE(1,9,N)
EXPERIENCE(6,1,S)
FAMILY(1,15,E)
FASHION(12,7,SW)
HAIRCUT(9,2,E)
HEALTH(3,13,N)
HORMONES(15,6,W)
JOINTS(15,14,NW)
LEISURE(7,14,W)
PENSION(2,1,S)
PETS(5,9,W)
POTIONS(9,7,SE)
RELATIONSHIPS(1,1,SE)
TRAVEL(3,9,SE)
VITAMINS(1,11,NE)

237

CONFUSION

Emergency: The surgeon is the boy's mother.

Bankrupt: He was playing monopoly

Asbo: He was on a bridge, almost at the other side it was quicker to carry on than to go back.

REBUS PUZZLES

MIND MATTER		= Mind over matter
OUT	LUNCH LUNCH LUNCH LUNCH	=Out for (4) lunch
TRANSLOSTATION		= Lost in translation

EMPTY NEST/FULL NEST SYNDROME

Birds of a Feather

A siege	of bitterns	A fling	of sandpipers
A bellowing	of bullfinches	An exultation	of skylarks
A wake	of buzzards	A wisp	of snipe
A clattering	of choughs	A ubiquity	of sparrows
A piteousness	of doves	A murmuration	of starlings
A convocation	of eagles	A muster	of storks
A drum	of goldfinches	A flight	of swallows
A bazaar	of guillemots	A gargle	of swans
A kettle	of hawks	A mutation	of thrushes
A watch	of nightingales	A raffle	of turkeys
A huddle	of penguins	A pitying	of turtledoves
An unkindness	of ravens	A descent	of woodpeckers
A parliament	of rooks		

WORDSEARCH: Empty Nest/Full Nest

```
+  +  +  +  R  D  F  +  +  +  +  +  L  E  P
+  +  +  E  +  A  A  +  +  +  +  A  +  R  L
P  R  S  +  M  +  +  U  +  +  U  +  +  U  E
A  T  O  I  +  +  Y  +  G  N  +  +  +  S  A
R  +  L  U  +  +  +  C  D  H  O  M  E  I  S
E  Y  +  T  T  +  +  R  A  +  T  +  +  E  U
N  +  +  +  I  I  Y  G  +  V  +  E  +  L  R
T  E  +  +  +  M  N  +  +  +  I  +  R  +  E
S  +  C  +  +  I  E  E  +  +  +  R  +  S  E
O  +  +  A  R  G  N  I  K  O  O  C  P  E  C
N  +  +  A  E  M  O  C  N  I  +  +  F  +  A
S  +  H  +  +  P  +  +  +  +  +  I  +  +  P
+  S  +  +  +  +  +  +  +  L  Y  O  J  S
+  +  +  +  +  +  H  O  B  B  I  E  S  +  +
+  +  +  +  +  +  +  +  +  +  +  +  +  +  +
```

(Over,Down,Direction)
COOKING(12,10,W)
DAUGHTERS(6,1,SE)
FAMILY(7,1,SW)
HOBBIES(7,14,E)
HOME(10,5,E)
INCOME(10,11,W)
JOY(14,13,W)
LAUNDRY(13,1,SW)
LEISURE(14,7,N)
LIFE(11,13,NE)
PARENTS(1,3,S)
PEACE(6,12,NW)
PLEASURE(15,1,S)
PRIVACY(13,10,NW)
REST(5,1,SW)
ROUTINE(2,3,SE)
SHARING(2,13,NE)
SONS(1,9,S)
SPACE(15,13,N)
TIME(4,6,SE)

SUDOKU

9	7	4	2	1	8	6	5	3
5	6	2	9	7	3	1	8	4
1	8	3	5	4	6	7	9	2
2	4	6	7	9	1	8	3	5
3	1	5	4	8	2	9	6	7
7	9	8	3	6	5	4	2	1
4	3	1	8	2	9	5	7	6
8	2	7	6	5	4	3	1	9
6	5	9	1	3	7	2	4	8

SUDOKU

8	3	6	5	2	4	9	1	7
9	1	5	3	8	7	2	4	6
2	4	7	1	6	9	5	8	3
7	2	3	9	4	8	1	6	5
5	9	8	6	1	3	4	7	2
1	6	4	2	7	5	8	3	9
6	7	9	8	5	1	3	2	4
3	8	2	4	9	6	7	5	1
4	5	1	7	3	2	6	9	8

KAKURO

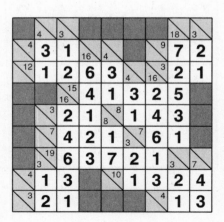

POST HOLIDAY BLUES

WORDSEARCH: Post Holiday blues

```
S P + + + + + + N + R + + S
S + I G N I I K S U + O + N +
E S + H S T A O B S + M I + +
N + U + S + + + + + A + + +
I + + R E D I S Y R T N U O C
P + + + F S N + + N + C + + +
P + + + T I + E U G A E + H +
A + + R + + N O I M N + + T +
H + O + + + M G P R + I + M +
T P D R I N K I N G F B T R +
S R W P L A N E S A H E + A +
+ + A O + G + + E O + A + W E
+ + + I N + + S T + + C + + +
+ + + + N S + E + + + H + + +
+ + + + + S L + + + + + + + +
```

(Over, Down, Direction)
BEACH(12,10,S)
BOATS(9,3,W)
CAMPING(12,6,SW)
COUNTRYSIDE(15,5,W)
DRINKING(3,10,E)
EATING(15,12,NW)
FRIENDSHIP(11,10,NW)
HAPPINESS(1,9,N)
HOTEL(11,11,SW)
MOUNTAINS(7,9,NE)
PLANES(4,11,E)
ROMANCE(12,1,S)
SEA(8,13,NE)
SKIING(9,2,W)
SNOW(6,14,NW)
SPORTS(1,11,NE)
SUN(10,3,N)
SURFING(2,3,SE)
TRAINS(1,10,SE)
WARMTH(14,12,N)

KAKURO

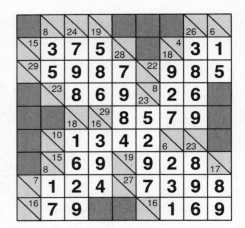

KAKURO

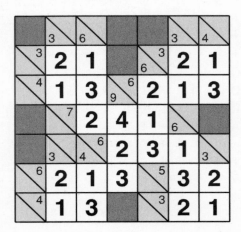

SUDOKU

9	2	5	4	3	7	6	1	8
6	3	8	2	1	9	5	7	4
7	1	4	6	5	8	3	2	9
3	9	7	5	6	4	1	8	2
5	6	1	7	8	2	4	9	3
4	8	2	1	9	3	7	5	6
1	4	3	8	2	5	9	6	7
2	7	6	9	4	1	8	3	5
8	5	9	3	7	6	2	4	1

REBUS PUZZLES

CAOT = Turncoat

LESS
MORE = Less is more

T T = Big Tease

DIET DISASTER

HANJIE

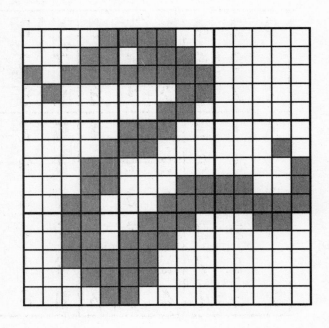

SUDOKU

9	2	4	3	7	5	1	8	6
1	8	5	6	4	9	7	3	2
6	7	3	2	1	8	9	5	4
8	1	2	9	5	4	6	7	3
5	3	6	8	2	7	4	9	1
7	4	9	1	3	6	5	2	8
3	9	8	7	6	1	2	4	5
4	6	7	5	8	2	3	1	9
2	5	1	4	9	3	8	6	7

HITORI

7	2	6	5	6	3	8	4
2	1	8	5	5	7	4	3
7	5	6	1	6	2	6	8
4	7	5	5	8	7	1	3
7	4	6	3	2	5	6	7
5	8	4	8	3	8	7	2
6	3	6	4	2	1	5	8
5	6	2	7	4	1	3	1

HANJIE

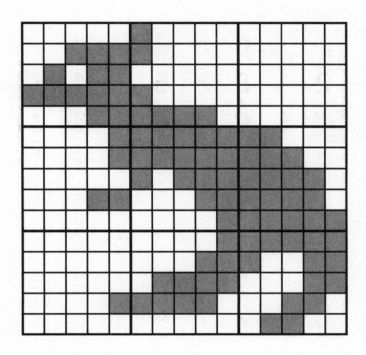

OUTSIDE THE BOX

Daylight Robbery
George is a baby.

Water, Water Everywhere
The woman has hiccoughs and the bartender thinks a shock will cure her faster than the water.

Double Decker
The child suggests letting some of the air out of the tyres.

WORDSEARCH: Diet Disaster

```
+  +  +  +  +  B  +  E  E  +  +  C  S  S
P  A  S  T  R  I  E  S  S  +  N  A  +  L  E
+  M  +  +  +  S  I  R  +  E  R  I  I  E  I
+  +  A  +  +  C  E  P  R  B  E  M  W  N  R
S  T  A  E  R  T  R  E  O  I  +  H  +  D  O
T  +  +  E  R  O  +  H  D  +  E  +  C  E  L
I  +  X  +  T  C  Y  +  +  S  +  S  +  R  A
U  E  +  E  +  D  E  T  A  L  O  C  O  H  C
R  +  I  +  R  +  +  C  D  W  A  T  E  R  N
F  N  +  A  +  +  +  E  I  H  S  I  F  +  U
+  +  T  +  +  +  N  T  +  +  +  +  +  +  T
+  E  +  +  +  O  +  I  +  +  +  +  +  +  S
S  +  +  +  T  +  +  F  +  +  +  +  +  +  +
+  +  +  +  +  +  +  +  +  +  +  +  +  +  +
```

(Over,Down,Direction)
BERRIES(6,1,SE)
CALORIES(15,8,N)
CARBOHYDRATES(13,1,SW)
CHEESE(13,6,NW)
CHOCOLATE(15,8,W)
EXERCISE(2,8,NE)
FISH(13,10,W)
FIT(8,13,N)
FRUIT(1,10,N)
ICE-CREAM(9,10,NW)
NUTS(15,9,S)
PASTRIES(1,2,E)
PROTEIN(8,4,SW)
SEEDS(6,3,SE)
SLENDER(14,1,S)
SLIM(15,1,SW)
TONED(5,13,NE)
TREATS(6,5,W;)
WATER(10,9,E)
WINE(13,4,NW)

251

THE END OF THE AFFAIR

WORDSEARCH: The end of the affair

```
+ + + E R L + D + P D + E J +
+ + V A E I I + I + E + T E +
+ O + T V S A H + N S + A Z +
L + T B T O S F W + S E N E +
+ E D A E D N O F + O N O B +
R + N E N A N A + A R T I E +
+ C + E T K U + S + C I S L +
E + I + N I M T + A + C S R +
+ R + U + + U Y I + C I A A +
F T E R C E S Q S F + N P T +
E M O S D N A H E T U G + S +
P O P U L A R + + R E L + + +
S E D U C T I V E + N R + + +
N O I T A N I G A M I U Y + +
+ + + + + + + + + + + + + + +
```

(Over,Down,Direction)
AFFAIR(10,6,NW)
BEAUTIFUL(4,4,SE)
CASANOVA(11,9,NW)
CROSSED(11,7,N)
DISTANCE(8,1,SW)
ENTICING(12,4,S)
FRIENDSHIP(1,10,NE)
HANDSOME(8,11,W)
IMAGINATION(11,14,W)
JEZEBEL(14,1,S)
LETTER(6,1,SW)
LOVE(1,4,NE)
MYSTERY(7,8,SE)
PASSIONATE(13,10,N)
POPULAR(1,12,E)
SECRET(7,10,W)
SEDUCTIVE(1,13,E)
STAR(14,11,N)
UNKNOWN(4,9,NE)
UNREQUITED(12,14,NW)

SUDOKU

3	4	1	7	5	6	8	2	9
2	6	9	4	8	3	7	1	5
5	8	7	9	2	1	6	4	3
7	5	2	1	6	9	3	8	4
6	1	8	3	4	5	9	7	2
9	3	4	2	7	8	1	5	6
1	7	6	5	3	2	4	9	8
8	9	5	6	1	4	2	3	7
4	2	3	8	9	7	5	6	1

HANJIE

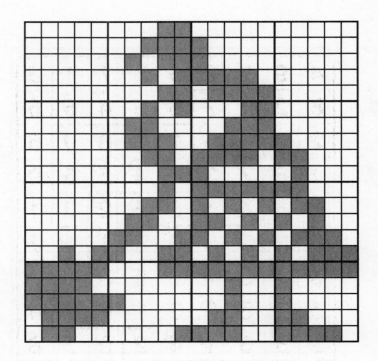

IRREGULAR SUDOKU

4	9	5	2	6	8	7	1	3
8	2	1	7	9	3	4	5	6
2	4	3	6	1	7	8	9	5
1	8	7	3	2	4	5	6	9
7	6	4	5	8	9	2	3	1
9	3	2	8	5	6	1	4	7
6	1	9	4	7	5	3	8	2
5	7	8	9	3	1	6	2	4
3	5	6	1	4	2	9	7	8

SLITHERLINK

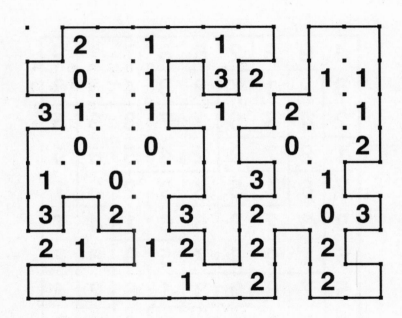